Praise for REAL *Top Producer*

REAL Top Producer by Chris Chopite is a great book for real estate agents who are interested in performing at the top of their game both personally and professionally. Chris's approach is real and relatable and highlights a comprehensive overview of what it takes to be successful in life and in business. What I found most valuable was his practical application within his teaching, especially in the realm of marketing, branding and professionalism. I highly recommend this book to anyone looking to take their real estate business to the next level with time-tested principles that can be easily applied by anyone at any experience level.

JAKE DIXON Founder and CEO of The Locker Room Coaching and Consulting, author and speaker

This book is going to help hundreds of thousands of realtors across the globe. *REAL Top Producer* is going to heavily impact their business! Great book to go through and have as a reference to all these concepts in one place.

SINA TAHAMI Director of Sales for the Vaughan Real Estate Advisors Top-Producing Team in Vaughan, Ontario, Canada

REAL Top Producer: Become a Top 1% Earner in Any Real Estate Market by Chris Chopite is an excellent resource for anyone interested in building a strong foundation to join an elite club of being in the top one percent in the real estate industry. The book is well-written and informative, and it provides a comprehensive overview of the branding, presence and marketing required to improve your business. What I found most valuable about this book was the importance of tracking your activities and business numbers in order to identify areas for improvement. I highly recommend this book to anyone looking to venture into the world of real estate as a salesperson, and even those that have just started or are seasoned and are looking to break through to find success.

ERIC MIRAFLOR Real estate professional in Toronto, Ontario, Canada

I love the graphics, tables and personal notes that you added—they generate rapprochement and confidentiality with the reader. I also love the personal stories. I think that for those who read it and are into the subject, it is almost a self-help book, where you offer, with great generosity, material and resources from a path that you have already traveled. It is, without a doubt, a very inspiring book for those who undertake this journey of becoming a REAL Top Producer one day. Congratulations!

ALICIA ERBITY Past real estate client of Chris (sold and bought with him)

REAL Top Producer is an excellent resource for anyone interested in real estate sales. The book is well-written and informative, and it provides a comprehensive overview of what it takes to become a top-producing real estate agent, including how to increase your productivity, branding, presence and marketing. It also covers key aspects such as looking within and understanding what is truly motivating you to become a Top Producer. I highly recommend this book to anyone looking to take their real estate career to the next level and truly be a REAL Top Producer.

ZACHARY BAKER Head of Talent Acquisition, Keller Williams Legacies Realty—fastest growing real estate brokerage in Vaughan, Ontario, Canada

Success is a journey fuelled by ambition. Ambition comes from our goals. Our goals come from our dreams. Our dreams are often inspired by the progressive individuals we surround ourselves with—Chris Chopite is that individual. This book chronicles his user-friendly guideline to work-life balance. He lays the foundation for successful self-marketing and management, reminding us of the importance of team building and investing in oneself. For those in the know it's a confirmation you're on the right path and for others it will get you on it. I highly recommend REAL *Top Producer* to any real estate professional looking for a roadmap that can bring them great success in their real estate business.

CAFFERY VANHORNE Award-winning stylist, designer and HGTV host

REAL *Top Producer* is an excellent resource for anyone interested in becoming a top producer in the real estate industry. The book is well-written, informative and provides a comprehensive overview of the importance of time management and structure, all while highlighting how sacrifice and courage can lead to your success. What I found most valuable about the book is how it relates to real life experiences and provides a unique point of view, which challenges the reader to look inwards to find their own success. I highly recommend this book to anyone looking to be successful, not just in real estate, but in their personal and professional life.

HASHIM ARTHUR Vice President of Operations, Global Real Estate Franchisor, founded in 1906

REAL
T⬆P
PRODUCER

BECOME A
TOP 1% EARNER
IN ANY REAL
ESTATE MARKET

GRAMMAR
FACTORY
— EST⁰ 2013 —

REAL TOP PRODUCER

CHRIS CHOPITE

REAL Top Producer
Copyright © 2024 by Chris Chopite.
All rights reserved.

Published by Grammar Factory Publishing, an imprint of MacMillan
Company Limited.

No part of this book may be used or reproduced in any manner whatso-
ever without the prior written permission of the author, except in the case
of brief passages quoted in a book review or article. All enquiries should
be made to the author.

Grammar Factory Publishing
MacMillan Company Limited
25 Telegram Mews, 39th Floor, Suite 3906
Toronto, Ontario, Canada
M5V 3Z1

www.grammarfactory.com

Chopite, Chris.
REAL Top Producer: Become a Top 1% Earner in Any Real Estate Market /
Chris Chopite.

Paperback ISBN 978-1-998756-52-0
eBook ISBN 978-1-998756-53-7

1. BUS054010 BUSINESS & ECONOMICS / Real Estate / Buying & Selling
Homes. 2. BUS058010 BUSINESS & ECONOMICS / Sales & Selling /
Management. 3. BUS043000 BUSINESS & ECONOMICS / Marketing /
General.

Production Credits
Cover design by Designerbility
Interior layout design by Setareh Ashrafologhalai
Book production and editorial services by Grammar Factory Publishing

Grammar Factory's Carbon Neutral Publishing Commitment
Grammar Factory Publishing is proud to be neutralizing the carbon
footprint of all printed copies of its authors' books printed by or ordered
directly through Grammar Factory or its affiliated companies through the
purchase of Gold Standard-Certified International Offsets.

Disclaimer
The material in this publication is of the nature of general comment only
and does not represent professional advice. It is not intended to provide
specific guidance for particular circumstances, and it should not be relied
on as the basis for any decision to take action or not take action on any
matter which it covers. Readers should obtain professional advice where
appropriate, before making any such decision. To the maximum extent
permitted by law, the author and publisher disclaim all responsibility
and liability to any person, arising directly or indirectly from any person
taking or not taking action based on the information in this publication.

For the woman who brought me into this world, the one who keeps me in it, the four children I've been blessed with, and the people who believed and continue to believe in me—this one, my first one, is for you.

CONTENTS

INTRODUCTION
WHAT IS A TOP PRODUCER?

IN AUGUST 2023 I was in Orlando, Florida, immersed in the buzzing atmosphere of the Breakthrough event hosted by the Locker Room, a leading coaching and training organization in the U.S. The room was full of brokers, real estate agents and industry leaders. I put up my hand, they gave me the mic, and I asked the question: "What is a Top Producer?" The responses, though diverse, painted a picture of uncertainty—ranging from being in the top ten percent of their brokerage to the elite five percent of their industry. Amid these varied definitions, a disconcerting truth emerged: The path to becoming a REAL Top Producer was wrapped in mystery.

I came to this event fully aware that nobody knew what a Top Producer was, because there is no straight answer to this question. The ambiguity made me wonder what makes someone a REAL Top Producer in this industry—what metrics are used to determine this title, and what does it truly mean?

I reflected on my experiences as a Top Producer to find a definition beyond metrics and numbers, one that spoke more deeply about what it means. But also, one that would satisfy those who really need a numerical explanation—a way to ask, "Am I or am I not a Top Producer? How do I know?"

A REAL Top Producer is a person who has built strong foundations for their business, has mastered their branding, presence and marketing (BPM), and has consistent, proven business results in the top one percent of their national industry average—regardless of who they pay their taxes to. Also, a REAL Top Producer knows to EDUCATE their clients; they don't "sell." Instead, they know their content, their product and their business so well that they're able to educate, and this client-education process organically "sells" a level of trust that propels the client to make a decision—an educated decision—and make a purchase.

So that's my definition—you must be in the top one percent in the nation, you must have mastered your business, and you must think of your core business not as *selling* to your clients, but as *educating* them. Now, how do you get there?

You must fight for the title of REAL Top Producer with courage, quality work and inspiration!

A Top Producer is more than a mere money-making machine. Financial success is crucial, but it only tells part of the tale. A Top Producer epitomizes the pinnacle of productivity, social responsibility and consistency, all while prioritizing quality. Most significantly, they serve as a source of inspiration—not only to themselves and those in their immediate circles but, importantly, to the emerging generation of leaders. This inspiration stems from their impactful actions and outstanding contributions to the industry they serve and the clients they represent.

After years of working towards becoming a Top Producer and finding my path to success, I decided I had to share the knowledge I have acquired to inspire others to transcend. This book will show you how to build your foundation, increase your BPM, and continue to improve the business.

"Self-discipline is the
ability to make yourself
do what you should do when
you should do it, whether
you feel like it or not."

BRIAN TRACY
Canadian-American motivational
speaker and world-renowned sales trainer

If you're reading this book, you already have the mindset for improvement; you want to know more and know you're destined for more. This book is the blueprint for becoming a Top Producer, so get ready to build your top-producing business!

Before we begin, there's one thing you need to do: you need to make a decision. You must decide that you want to be a Top Producer. You have to decide right now that you want to be an expert in your field and a leader to the people in your world—and that extends beyond your business.

Once you decide, you have to have the self-discipline to continue on your path to becoming a Top Producer. If you don't have that discipline, you have deceived yourself—you, the most important person in your entire life!

This book is about awareness, self-discovery, and life structure; it is not just a how-to book. It includes timeless advice, methods and secrets to building a strong foundation and systems for your business and life. Let's have a look at what's in store as you read.

Part one: Foundation— Preparation, Planning & Time

The first three critical chapters lay the foundation for your business. It's a deep dive into the purpose and the significant "why" behind your endeavours. The challenge lies in resisting the urge for immediate results. Your commitment to sacrifice, building a strategic plan, and mastering time-blocking and scheduling form the pillars of this foundational stage. This is the bedrock upon which your success will rest.

Part two: Creation—Brand, Presence & Marketing

Moving into Part two, we explore the essence of your business—your brand, presence and marketing. Here, we guide you through building a powerful brand, refining your professional presence, and mastering effective marketing strategies. You will get creative and supercharge your journey to becoming a REAL Top Producer.

Part three: Elevation— Tools, Tracking & Team

The final three chapters bring it all together and outline the indispensable tools that will empower you to rise to the ranks of the industry's top one percent. Learn how to refine your systems and processes, track your progress, and build a phenomenal team to help you, all while implementing the secret business hacks that will get you farther faster.

In my first year in real estate, I made a whopping $28,000. Hah! But by year five I had built a brand around my name, and with the quality of my work and exceptional service I provided my clients I became the #2 real estate salesperson at my brokerage. I was making well over $400,000 a year and this allowed me to secure my family, fund other business endeavours and earn a spot in the top one percent of income earners in all of Canada's real estate sales industry. Now it's time to pay it forward and pass on the hard-earned lessons from that journey.

This is your moment to decide; to commit to becoming a Top Producer. Let's embark on this journey together—a journey that transcends mere techniques and endures as a timeless guide I know you will return to for decades.

Let's begin.

PART ONE

FOUNDATION

PREPARATION, PLANNING & TIME

HERE'S A **REAL** STORY...

It's Sunday morning. My schedule says: 4:45 am—wake up, then power up and plan the following week. Sundays are my family days, but sometimes the family doesn't get up too early and I have a little more time to work on the business.

This particular Sunday, it's quiet. All I hear is the furnace going... I feel inspired and decide, "I need to review my gameplan to ensure my life is in alignment with my current plans and updated desires."

I go to the living room and open up my board—yes, I have a five-foot wide white board in my living room that I use to visualize my plans, ideas, concepts and thoughts. I go to the board and I begin.

I list everything out. This year: thirty-six transactions, twelve listings, twenty-four buyers. I spend time looking at it and visualizing everything with an awkward stare—a stare that sometimes concerns my kids—but they know I'm in the zone. I make notes as I go along; get my newsletter done. I set my priorities: write down the three most important things I need to accomplish; hire an assistant by April 5th; go to four events by November 30th; build my database to 2,000 by December 20th. And then I sit there and visualize what those priorities can do for my business WHEN, not IF, I accomplish them.

Thirty-five to forty minutes into it, my daughter comes down and sees me writing on the board. I'm still refining my plan. She says good morning and passes by me to go do her own morning work. I step back, read everything I wrote and smile—YES, I've got it... I know what I need to do.

This early morning planning was, and is, something I do often. As a Top Producer, visualizing the game plan, writing it out, then rewriting it and expanding it has always been something that resets my thoughts and provides clarity for my weekly plan of attack. In fact, in my night table drawer I keep a notebook with ideas and monthly objectives that I check off once completed, or cross out if they're not required any longer. If an item is not completed, there's also a quick explanation of why—just in case I need to jog my memory if I later wonder why it was not done. Side note—sometimes you WILL have an objective that, two or three months ago, you thought was a great objective to have or goal to achieve. But, through growth, experience and further education, you see that there's a better way or a more important objective to focus on. This happens; don't stress too much about it, just know you're normal! Lol

All of the above is what I do to stay tight with my vision. To remind myself of the sacrifices I need to make and what's at stake. Constantly looking at the plan, and rewriting and tweaking it as I grow and become wiser, keeps me on track.

If you're clear on the plan, you will understand what the best use of your time is, and where you can utilize any spare time you have to potentially get ahead and double down on the process. I have always been visual—that explains why I have a five-foot whiteboard in my living room! And being visual, I'm always "presenting" to myself—selling myself on my own thoughts first. If I can't believe in something or get behind it, I know it's not a good idea and I need to come back to the drawing board (literally) and start retooling the plan until it moves me—until that feeling of "I can't wait to start" takes over. You know that feeling?

Planning and preparation are critical. You need to prepare your mind, prepare your plan and plan your time. Without this foundation, you will struggle to become a Top Producer. That's what the first part of this book is all about. Here we go!

CHAPTER 1

SACRIFICE & COURAGE

"He who is not courageous enough to
take risks will accomplish nothing in life."

MUHAMMAD ALI

Legendary American professional boxer,
Olympic gold medalist and social activist

WELL, WE start with the ugly. I like to always begin by bursting bubbles and checking to see if, right from the get-go, you have the grit to take the gut punches and uphill battles that ALL future Top Producers must overcome to get to the top.

In this chapter, we will dive into the meaning of sacrifice, why you need to become comfortable with it, and why this is not such a bad thing. Then, in the second half of the chapter, we'll look at courage. Because, if you're going to become a REAL Top Producer, you will need to muster your courage.

Sacrifice

Let me tell you a story about sacrifice...

My wife is committed to being at home and providing unwavering support, guidance, and accountability to our four children. To do this, she has sacrificed her own wish to have a career, make her own money, and build closer relationships with her friends. She has had to relinquish her desire to take interesting classes, be more social, and meet new people. She has had to give up being the adventurous person she was prior to starting a family. She understood that in order to have the larger family she wanted, she had to sacrifice—until our kids have grown—the free life she once had.

In addition to that sacrifice there are the natural frustrations of family life. Tsunamis of energy and chaos take place every morning in our household. Then, in the evening, the second "shift" begins and my wife has to make dinner, ensure the kids do their homework, then clean up the kitchen as the kids waltz up the stairs and take two hours to shower and get to bed. It'll be 10.00 pm before she has any down time, 11.00 pm before she gets to bed, and she has to do it all again the next day... seven days straight. You get my drift?

The question is: why does she do this? Because the vision of what she's fighting for in the future—healthy, smart, socially responsible kids—is more rewarding than what she is giving up in the present. The sacrifice and the pain are worth it. It's a sacrifice that goes beyond traditional notions. It's about dedicating time, effort, and a physical presence to nurture our children into responsible societal contributors. It's a profound sacrifice that requires getting comfortable with the challenges that come with it and embracing the pain for a greater purpose.

And you may ask, "Well, what does that have to do with being a TOP Producer?" It's a two-part thing. The first part is about the fact that there are all sorts of sacrifices in life and everyone must make them. The second part is that sacrifice is part of business. So, get used to it.

This is also partly a HUGE tip of my hat to my wife for all the hard work she does to ensure we, as a family, have some sort of order: *Baby, I know we're not perfect, but I SO appreciate your sacrifice and constant effort to keep us all moving forward. Love you.*

Ok, back to the book...

It's not easy, but it is a choice... You have to CHOOSE to be in the moment, accept the sacrifice that is being made and get comfortable with the process. Huge hack: We stay grateful, we don't HAVE to raise children, we GET TO raise children... there's a difference. For you, you don't HAVE to be in real estate sales, you GET TO be in real estate sales. Not only this, you get to train and work toward becoming a REAL Top Producer and enjoy a life that others only dream of.

Trade-offs: What's your offering?

In life, we must make sacrifices for the things we want. You should plan what you're willing to offer up for success. The benefit of identifying your sacrifices before you embark on your journey to becoming a Top Producer is that it allows you to set the sturdiest foundation possible. Your foundation must withstand both personal and business earthquakes. If you begin this journey with a weak foundation, or if you've started this journey without considering that sacrifices must be made, you stand the chance of cracking your mental and business foundation at the first sign of stress.

Let's start by analyzing your life: make a list of time wasters—the things you're willing to give up to make more time to work on your business. But a word of warning: do not give up EVERYTHING for success—that is a quick way to be miserable. The best way to figure out what should and should not be sacrificed is to look at your time wasters and non-negotiables. Once those time wasters are off your list, you'll be left with ONLY the non-negotiables.

Time wasters and non-negotiables will be different for everyone. In my case, for example, I have made a conscious choice to minimize—not omit completely, just minimize—family outings and gatherings. Family time is something that I enjoy, but that I've had to sacrifice to have time to do other things that are a greater priority. I mention family because it's the one thing that has the potential to throw us off course. It's SO important, but because we are emotionally involved with our families, family life can get the better of us if we don't consciously control it. So, I only attend significant family events; not ALL of them. As the provider for my family, I believe there are better uses for my time that will ultimately uplift us all, even if that means a bit of familial sacrifice.

Now, don't misunderstand me here. I WANT to spend ultra-special moments with my family—just not ALL my time with my family. In fact, I actually LIKE missing my family. There's a level of appreciation you gain by missing something. In a nutshell, it's about balance—too much of anything is not good.

There is never enough time to do everything in life, but there is always enough time to do the right thing. Therefore, I have made it a non-negotiable not to mess with my fitness regimens and eating habits. This matters to me; maintaining good habits helps with my energy and allows me to show up strong and vital and as an asset to any meeting, event, or coaching session.

I recommend you make a list of trade-offs and non-negotiables, review it weekly, and ensure that the things you're spending your time on are a high priority and moving you towards your goals and vision. If they're not, remove them from your calendar. Your list should be specific and each "offering" should have a small note to clarify what's involved. Anything vague is untrackable; no details equals no clarity. If you can't describe it well, you can't visualize it, and you won't be able to follow it.

Let's take a look at my offerings to show you what I mean.

My sacrifice list:

1   **I will offer up all TV shows**. I will only watch sports—but NO full games; only ten-minute highlights.

2   **I will offer up Saturday night with the boys—OR only attend events if my wife and kids can be with me.** I will only go out with the boys four times per year; once every three months.

3   **I will not clean my car anymore.** I will teach my son how to clean my car, show him how to do a great job; then, I will pay him to do the job and teach him how to invest his money.

4   **I will sacrifice late nights and sleeping in.** I will wake up at 4:45 am and go to bed at 9:00 pm. This strict regimen allows me to start every day at the highest level of energy and productivity possible.

As you make your list, consider that anything that doesn't bring you joy, money or fulfillment is not worth your time. Happiness is critical. We will never be able to get away from the fact that we, the human race, need to feel wanted, fulfilled, and appreciated.

What brings you joy and happiness? Know this as you make your list and, in the same breath, know that ALL should be about joy. Be clear on what you're willing to give

"Embrace the suck, embrace the sacrifice, name your sacrifices; if you do that, the doing part gets easy."

ALEX HORMOZI
author of *$100M leads*,
speaker and centi-millionaire

up, but know the difference between things that are tempo-rary joy and things that are truly going to fulfil you and make a difference in your life.

Friends and family: Release the emotional handcuff

I explained how my wife sacrificed building friendships to give her time to raise strong, healthy, happy children. And I also explained how I made the decision to not go to every family gathering. These were tough choices. Resisting family gatherings, declining invitations from friends, and sacrific-ing beloved activities is challenging. When you encounter resistance from family and friends, stay steadfast in your commitment. Friends and family may express concerns and say things like "You're moving on," or "We don't see you around anymore," but remember, moments of isolation are part of your journey toward success. Embrace this as part of your growth, recognizing that while friends may perceive you differently, your unwavering focus on your goals is cru-cial for you to live the life you envision. Remember, your family and your true friends will always be there for you. And if they REALLY care for you and your aspirations, they will encourage your absence as you work toward accom-plishing your goals.

Family holds immense importance in my life, and my upbringing was marked by a strong family bond. This pro-found connection motivates my hard work—a dedication driven by the desire to create a future where we can rel-ish more moments together as a family. I envision being a supportive presence for my family's needs and giving them enriching experiences. While it might be challeng-ing to articulate these intentions to everyone, I find it more effective to maintain focus on the actionable steps I've com-mitted to. Rather than telling them about my goals, I prefer showing them through tangible results. The commitment is in the doing, and I believe that my actions and achievements will eloquently convey the depth of my dedication to my family and goals.

Delayed gratification: the essential sacrifice

I said before that what each of us chooses to sacrifice and what our non-negotiables are will be different. But there is one thing that all Top Producers must sacrifice—instant gratification.

We all want results. And most of us want them NOW! We've all got way too used to instant gratification in modern society. Social media has a lot to answer for here. But if you can't delay gratification—that is, sacrifice feeling good in the moment for the promise of a better future—you won't succeed.

Embracing the power of delayed gratification is a key principle often emphasized by Tony Robbins. It involves resisting the allure of instant rewards in favour of anticipating greater gains in the future. It's not merely an exercise in self-control, but a potent tool for living a purpose-driven life. Studies indicate a strong link between delayed gratification, impulse control, and overall life success.

So how do you do this? How do you learn to delay gratification? Your secret weapon here is to focus on the process, not the end goal. Let's unpack this a little further...

Whether your goal is a sale, a listing, or monetary gains, if you focus solely on that, the journey becomes an emotional rollercoaster. Learning to embrace the process, rather than fixating on results, is a game-changer. I want you to fall in love with the journey, the daily grind that leads to success. Unlike waiting for things to unfold, focusing on the process empowers you to control your actions, and creates a sense of peace and predictability in your business. Confidence follows suit as your plans materialize, creating a smoother path

"Delayed gratification means resisting the temptation of an immediate reward, in anticipation that there will be a greater reward later."

TONY ROBBINS
Motivational speaker and a
global inspirational force

to success. The true victory lies in accomplishing what you set out to do daily, emphasizing the importance of a well-defined process and setting achievable targets (more on this in Chapter 4).

Remember to celebrate your daily activities, weekly efforts, and monthly milestones, valuing the journey as much as the ultimate results. Establishing milestones and associating gratifying moments with each achievement creates a structured framework. This practice is important because, without a clear plan, individuals can find themselves at the mercy of their impulses. Without a defined vision or mission, you'll find yourself winging it and delaying gratification indefinitely. This is unsustainable, so again, make sure to acknowledge and celebrate your small achievements.

Courage

Let me tell you a story about courage...

It was 2013. I had two children, both still toddlers under the age of three. Ty and Sienna were best friends, and it was so touching to see how Ty took such great care of her. I had three jobs—I was working as a building inspector during the day, parking cars as a valet attendant at night, and working security at a nightclub on Saturday nights.

I was sacrificing my time to work three jobs and I needed to do it in order to support my family. I worked over 100 hours a week and made just over $80,000. At that time in my life, it was essential; I had to do it—but I knew it WAS NOT sustainable.

Then, one night, parking cars in the freezing cold and getting $2.00 tips, I pulled a piece of paper out of my pocket. Then and there, I wrote down my goals and my plans for the year. I kept reminding myself that where I was and what I was doing was NOT going to define who I would become—there was 100% going to be a better life for me. At that time, I had to do what I was doing, but I also had to believe that this was just a stop-gap, a frozen (literally) moment in time that would soon become just a page in the book of my success—and so it was.

The courage mindset

There is no sacrifice without courage. Delaying gratification and making sacrifices today for a better future takes courage. The courage mindset is the knowledge that in order to achieve greatness you must do something that scares you. The courage mindset is also the knowledge that everything negative that may come is the path to success and, in your case, to becoming a REAL Top Producer. The courage mindset is not something you're born with, but something you can create with daily training, and through accepting that fear is a good thing. When you're scared and you do it anyway is precisely when you unlock the courage mindset. And when you do this, you can accomplish so much more in life.

The courage mindset unlocks a higher power of self. It allows you to overcome self-doubt, competitors and naysayers, and gives your mind the ability to think in terms of abundance. A lot of the time, we're the ones who get in the way of greatness. Unlock your courage mindset and get out of your own way!

Have faith

Believing in something is a form of courage. When you genuinely believe in something you don't necessarily see, but trust that it is there, that's a form of courage.

What I want to tell you is that if you have faith in yourself and your business, you will believe, you will know, that you can be better. Like believing in a higher power you cannot see, you will just *know* that you're destined for more. This is the courage I want you to find—this belief, this idea that you do not need to SEE the money and all the tangibles... yet. But you need to have the courage to know you are destined for more, for a better life, and to impact more people. What an amazing thought... the thought that you can live the life you want through this incredible career of real estate sales.

Have the courage to believe in yourself, and the results will come. One, because it HAS been done before you, but more importantly because you're taking the steps, both mentally and physically, to accomplish what you desire. Have faith in your ability, see yourself where you want to be, and then act—find the tools and the people to help you get to what you envision.

It all starts with courage and believing in yourself. Have faith, it will happen.

Get comfortable with pain

Courage allows you to endure the inevitable pain that you will experience on your journey to becoming a REAL Top Producer. There will be growth, pleasure and improvement only after there has been pain. Growth is uncomfortable. Consider going to the gym. Your muscle ONLY grows when you damage it a little bit by creating microtears. It's uncomfortable, but you tear the muscle a little bit, it grows back stronger, then you go and tear it again... and it re-builds, bigger and better.

Now, to the gym enthusiast—I'm not saying you should go and work out until you get a grade three muscle strain and completely rupture the muscle. Let's take it in context here—the point I'm raising is that as you go on in your professional real estate sales career, you will experience discomfort, strain and pain. IT IS NORMAL, so lean into it! You're fine—stay focused on the why and stay committed to the daily tasks. You got this!

Pain is a good sign. Don't quote me here, but as I tell my daughter Sienna when we're training for her track and field meets, "Pain is weakness leaving the body." She always laughs, but she gets it—it's painful, but it's this exact pain that will give her the satisfaction of a better time around the track, a better placement in her race, and with that, the ultimate reward—winning, achieving, accomplishing.

Eat your obstacles

Courage is all in your head and in your mind; it's a mindset. You must encourage your mind to think that you are capable of so much more, and that obstacles are only there to prove that you can overcome them.

See your obstacles as the mushrooms in *Mario Brothers*. Every time you eat an obstacle (a mushroom) you get bigger and stronger. But in real life, unlike *Mario Brothers*, you don't go back down to miniature Mario, you stay the same size and get even bigger and stronger when you eat the next obstacle.

So, look at obstacles as an opportunity to become bigger, stronger, smarter, better, more capable of survival. Make yourself this promise: as of today, you will seek obstacles, because every time you jump over them, solve them and "eat them," you will be better. You will be rewarded with more opportunities, impact more people and become more and more unstoppable. You are more than your obstacles and your obstacles are the way!

The sacrifice & courage lifecycle

Sacrifice takes courage and courage means sacrifice. Together, these qualities create their own lifecycle. There is no success, no greatness, no top of the mountain, without climbing it. And climbing it comes with shortness of breath, a few bruises and a ton of obstacles.

However, it's not all gloom and fear; For all this courage and sacrifice will yield great wins that will carry you toward the next step, which will yield yet more obstacles that must be overcome with courage and sacrifice... and then it repeats! For how long, I hear you wonder...

No, I cannot tell you exactly how long it takes to get to the top of the mountain. That would be predicting your future, and I'm not a fortune teller. Here's what I WILL tell you: after courage and sacrifice comes the reward, a moment of accomplishment. There is a moment when you fall to your knees and say, "Wow, thank you God, we did it!" (Note: you'll be more trained to recognize and enjoy the win if you consistently train yourself to be grateful for the little things. When you do this, the big wins are going to be so much more enjoyable and worth every bead of sweat, clawing scar and bruised eye!)

Courage is NOT about being fearless—courage is about recognizing your fears and facing them.

Let's make courage a CHOICE: choose to be courageous. Exercise your courage daily to help build it up!

"The more we are able to face our fears, the more we will replace fear-based responses with courageous ones. But it's not all about a struggle with the inner enemy. For as we fight our fear, we will find ourselves acting in ways that make us feel more alive."

MANFRED F.R. KETS DE VRIES
psychoanalyst, consultant and
professor of leadership development

CHAPTER SUMMARY

To become a REAL Top Producer, you will have to make sacrifices. Some of those sacrifices will be hard, but know that they will pay for themselves over and over again when you finally make it to the top. Work out your time wasters and non-negotiables and stick to your plan—this will ensure you don't offer up the wrong things. One of the sacrifices you must make is the instant joy of a quick win. You must learn delayed gratification if you're going to stay the course.

Courage is key. There will be obstacles, but you must feel the fear and do it anyway, as the saying goes. Learn to embrace obstacles for the opportunities they are to grow and become stronger. Have faith in yourself and the path, and know that the sacrifice and courage lifecycle, when you invite it into your life, will lead you to the success you desire.

6 ⌁ TAKEAWAYS

- Make a list of your time wasters and non-negotiables.

- Be willing to sacrifice.

- Seek obstacles, because every time you overcome one you will be better: be rewarded with more opportunities; impact more people; and become more and more unstoppable.

- Courage is NOT about being fearless—courage is about recognizing your fear and then strategizing mentally to act, plan and execute!

- There will be growth, joy and improvement when there's pain. Pain precedes growth!

- The more we are able to face our fears, the more we will replace fear-based responses with courageous ones.

ARE YOU A **REAL** TOP PRODUCER?

Find out:

Get your RTP Rating now! Take the assessment
to find out if you are currently a REAL Top Producer,
and if not, what you're missing to get there:

chrischopite.com/REALTopProducer/Assessment

CHAPTER 2

BUILD YOUR PLAN

*"One hour of planning can save
you ten hours of DOING!"*

DALE CARNEGIE
Educator, thought leader and author

WELCOME TO what I consider the most impactful and crucial chapter on your journey to success. The significance of starting with a well-thought-out plan cannot be overstated, and I'm excited to share why. Countless professionals, leaders, and influential Top Producers attribute their success to the critical step of crafting a vision and a plan. Whether scribbled on paper, typed on a computer, or displayed on a white board, the transformational power of manifesting your vision in tangible form is unparalleled.

In the whirlwind of life, fast-paced challenges will come at you from all directions, and relying solely on your memory can be a dangerous practice. In Chapter 1, we got you into the right headspace, and this chapter marks the starting point of your structured plan of action, an essential ingredient of success. It's about constructing your planning portfolio—a comprehensive toolset that includes a GPS, a

5-3-1, and a vision and mission board. These elements work synergistically as the foundation of your success journey.

This strategic approach is the key to unlocking a clear path and vision toward monumental greatness and success. Get ready to embark on a transformative journey, and let's build the foundation for your extraordinary future together.

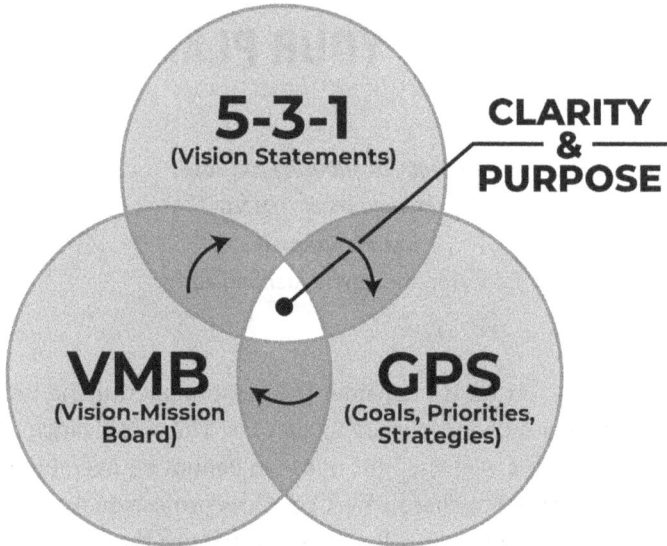

FIGURE 2.1 Planning portfolio

Build your GPS

Navigating the journey of success without a clear destination is similar to driving without setting your GPS coordinates. Just as a GPS guides us precisely to our desired endpoint, a REAL Top Producer's GPS encompasses goals, priorities and strategies. In this section, we'll learn how to construct your GPS. This tool has been a steadfast anchor for many on their path to becoming Top Producers. Writing down your goals is a fundamental step, an essential requirement for anyone aspiring to REAL Top Producer status. It's not just a task, it's a powerful directive that signals your subconscious to resolve challenges and seek solutions throughout your journey.

Building your GPS involves identifying a unifying goal that will be your focal point for the year, coupled with a strategic plan outlining how you will achieve it.

The benefits of this structured approach are vast, and include:

- Enhanced focus,
- More efficient use of your time, and
- Greater clarity.

Some people make the mistake of skipping this step. This leads to risks such as divided effort and a lack of clarity. Don't be one of those people! Instead, embrace the profound impact it can have on streamlining your path to success, ensuring a journey marked by focus, clarity and fulfillment.

Let's get started.

The G—Goal

According to wise and wonderful Gary Keller, the key is to identify that singular goal which, if achieved, will pave the way for everything else you desire in life.

There's nothing unclear about a goal—it's either accomplished or not. In identifying that goal, also identify what drives you toward it—the mighty force of your WHY.

My WHY is to leave the world a better place than it was when I came into it. I do this by ensuring I teach my kids to be givers, not takers. In my business, I achieve this by helping realtors achieve their highest and best potential, thus ensuring we change the way the world sees and interacts with real estate professionals. This is the beginning of creating a level of respect and appreciation similar to how doctors, engineers and firefighters are regarded and respected.

My WHY is so big that I will probably need to live 300 years to accomplish it! It's bigger than me. It's more important than me. It keeps me up at night. It drives me to learn, to be better and to constantly improve. You need something that does the same to you.

What is one unifying goal that you'll focus on throughout the year? This is the main question you must ask yourself. It starts with the ONE thing you want to achieve.

The P—Priorities

Priorities are the driving force; the tasks that, once accomplished, will yield the results you're looking for, thus accomplishing the goal—your ONE thing.

As a REAL Top Producer, your priorities are almost always based on some sort of business-generating activities. For example, one priority when I was in real estate sales and what I see now among current Top Producers is conversations. Conversations with the goal of booking appointments. Because once you have appointments you can get contracts signed, and once you have a contract signed you finally have the opportunity to generate some revenue.

More significant priorities I've seen in recent years are adding people to the database and conducting social-media/ marketing campaigns. Consider adding ten people to your database daily as a SMART priority—measurable and specific. Achieving nine out of ten is a daily miss; repeated shortfalls could lead to a significant setback by year-end. Unlike strategies that may evolve, priorities stay steadfastly connected to the goal and rarely shift unless the goal transforms.

When we say priorities, we mean tasks that are an absolute PRIORITY. These elements have a measurable impact. Once set, this list becomes your daily North Star. It demands intense focus and requires daily tracking. Tracking priorities is your daily checkpoint, crucial for acknowledging and celebrating those small victories. Recognize that these everyday triumphs are the building blocks of monumental success. REAL Top Producers excel at winning every day; they grasp the art of staying motivated and inspired by systematically accomplishing their daily priorities. With unwavering commitment, they pursue their daily goals, adeptly identifying deviations, knowing when to recalibrate, and recognizing the moments to seek support, coaching and guidance.

For me, the number one thing was always conversations. Honestly, everything else is secondary. As my good friend and real estate leader Jake Dixon says, real estate is a contact sport—it's time to get your jersey dirty!

The S—Strategies

Implementing strategies is a fascinating part of this journey. Along the way, you'll be battling up hills and negotiating your way around cliffs. You need to look ahead and establish the safest course of action. You must build bridges to see you safely across the challenges in your path. You need to set up checkpoints as part of your strategy, where you will pause and take a fresh look at your priorities—are you achieving forward momentum?

But don't be impatient—it's not uncommon to believe you've nailed the right strategy only to discover that there might be a more effective approach. However, you should exercise caution; switching strategies too soon could mean missing out on striking gold. To avoid this pitfall, you must fact-check and cross-reference your strategy with the experiences of those who've trodden the path before you. This ensures that when you commit to a specific strategy, you do so with confidence in its effectiveness and an understanding of the timeline for tangible results.

So, to summarize: your WHY is the fuel for the vehicle; you, the driver or the team, represent the executors of the whole vision, and the vehicle embodies the strategy and tools that will propel you toward that destination.

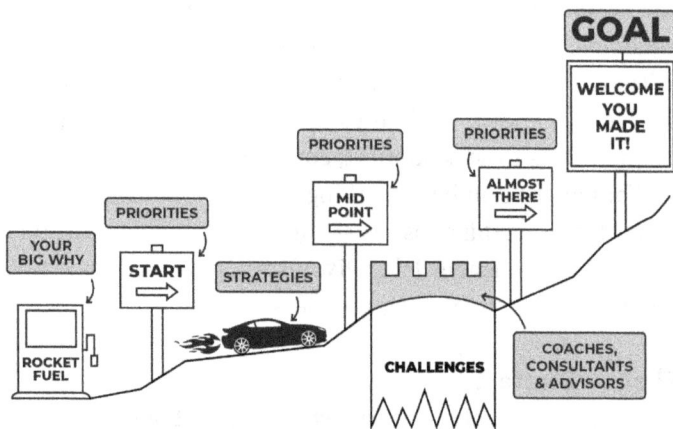

FIGURE 2.2 The GPS

Your GPS is an indispensable tool for your business. Our model is straightforward; clarity is the linchpin. It's about being direct and saying it in plain English. Your understanding of this entire process should be so clear that you could explain it to an eight-year-old.

If you want to access my GPS Builder, head to chrischopite .com/RTP and you'll find it under resources. This tool will give you and your team crystal-clear guidance on your business path, and its versatility extends beyond professional goals to personal aspirations. The key is to document your goals, make them visual, print them out, and revisit them regularly, if not daily!

Prepare your 5-3-1

In the journey toward success, envisioning the future is your compass, and the 5-3-1 framework acts as your guiding light. Embrace the power of planning; in five years, you can achieve the extraordinary. This simple yet profound exercise involves summarizing your fifth, third and first years into a clear vision. Yes, it involves writing, but putting your aspirations on paper gives your mind the clarity it craves and transforms your plans into a vivid reality.

The benefits of this approach include:

- **Inspiration**: Ignite a fire within by visualizing your future achievements.

- **Direction**: Provide your mind with a clear path to follow.

- **Connection**: Know your 'WHY' and reconnect with the driving force behind your endeavours.

- **Clarity**: Transform your dreams into tangible, achievable goals.

The risks of failing to take this approach include:

- **No direction**: Without a plan, you may wander aimlessly.

- **No inspiration**: Lack of a clear vision can lead to a loss of motivation.

- **No reason**: The crucial why behind your actions may become unclear.

Okay, that should have convinced you that you need to do this. Now here's how to do it!

The five-year plan

Let's do some self-discovery and goal setting as you create a vivid picture of your life five years from today. In this exercise, we explore the life you envision in terms of income, lifestyle, family, philanthropy, and personal fulfillment.

Picture yourself in the driver's seat of your life, navigating the roads of success. Write a plan rich with details, capturing the essence of the life you aspire to. Imagine the impact of your success on every aspect of your existence.

Here are a few things you might want to consider when you're writing your five-year plan:

- Envision your income, mapping out the financial milestones you aim to achieve. What does financial success look like to you?

- Paint a picture of your daily life—what car graces your driveway, what activities are your children involved in, and what is the overall quality of your family life?

- Outline where and how you contribute to causes close to your heart. How are you investing your time and resources to make a positive impact?

- Describe the daily routines and activities that contribute to your personal development and overall well-being.

- Outline your workweek—how many days a week do you work, and how many free days do you get to enjoy? Imagine a life where work and personal pursuits harmonize seamlessly.

This exercise isn't about wishful thinking; it's about turning your dreams into tangible, achievable goals. Let your imagination loose, but keep within the bounds of reality and steer clear of grandiose fantasies. Keep your plan to 750 words.

The three-year plan

Now let's explore your three-year plan, the midpoint between now and five years in the future. Follow the rules and prompts in your five-year plan, but now imagine what your life will look like in three years. Paint a vivid picture not just of your external achievements, but also of the emotional landscape. This exercise, far more consequential than any sports event or client meeting, empowers your subconscious mind to tirelessly work toward manifesting the reality you envision. Again, keep your plan to 750 words.

The one-year plan

Get ready to breathe life into the goal outlined on your GPS; this plan will create a vibrant picture of your first year working toward becoming a REAL Top Producer. Dive deep into the narrative—express the sacrifices you're willing to make and spotlight the priorities demanding your attention. Don't shy away from detailing your success celebrations. Envision the places you'll go, the heartfelt gifts for your family, and the investments or experiences for those close to you. Whether it's a special getaway, meaningful purchases, or gestures of gratitude, every word in this plan brings your remarkable journey to life. Manifest your greatness through the power of your story. The same rule of just 750 words applies.

And now for a quick side note: As you can tell, I love planning! In fact, I could plan all day, but my editor told me this chapter was getting too long and I had to stop adding to it. Anyway, if you love planning too and want to do some more, head to chrischopite.com/RTP, where you can find a guide to planning for your retirement, and also a guide to reviewing your plan with your significant other.

Create your vision and mission board

The final step in creating your plan is to create an inspiring visual of your ultimate goal—a Vison and Mission Board (VMB). This is a visual representation of your dreams that will serve as a constant reminder and encouragement to stay the course and stick to your plan. But it isn't a mere collage; it's a masterpiece, a work of art that encapsulates your dreams and propels you toward a future of abundance.

The benefits of creating a VMB include:

- **Direction**: You have a clear path to follow.

- **Visual reference**: Being able to SEE your goals provides a tangible reminder of your dreams.

- **Excitement**: Your VMB is a source of daily inspiration.

- **Sharing and conversation**: A tool for engaging with others and an opportunity to ask for help.

The risks of not creating a VMB include:

- **No excitement**: The spark may die without a constant reminder.

- **No momentum**: Without the VMB, there is no fuel.

- **Forgetting your WHY**: Without the art as your constant reminder, your WHY can be lost.

- **Distractions and lack of focus**: Life happens, and without a VMB it can take over.

Now let's have a look at how to go about creating your vision and mission board.

The artistic weekend ritual

Dedicate a full weekend or a Saturday to this activity, and involve your family if possible. You can take either a physical or digital approach—in recent years, the digital option has offered incredible flexibility. You can create a dedicated folder on Google Drive for your vision board. Alternatively, you could go the old-fashioned way and create a dedicated portfolio for this task—you're starting with a blank slate here.

In creating your VMB, make sure you ignite your creative spark:

- Embrace your inner creative child and let your imagination run wild. There are no rules; it's a personal journey.

- Ensure your artwork evokes the emotions tied to your daily struggles and aspirations. It's a visual cue of the greatness you're destined to achieve.

- Let it be a powerful motivator; a symbol that teases you out of bed, rekindling the fire within.

Now here's what you should include:

- Ensure your Big WHY is visually represented; let it be a constant reminder of your profound motivation, whether it's an image or a symbol.

- Integrate your goals into the artwork creatively. For instance, if your goal is thirty-six transactions, include a symbolic representation of that—like the number thirty-six next to an image of a flourishing tree, embodying growth.

- Don't shy away from depicting your sacrifices. Your VMB should be a vivid reminder of what you're willing to endure for your dreams.

- Create a visual representation of your dreams: Envision the car, the house, the cottage, the dream vacation. Make them tangible through images. Use words that resonate deeply, such as COURAGE, INTEGRITY, GROWTH, HEALTH and GOD. Get creative with their visual representation, making each element a part of your unique story.

A picture truly is worth a thousand words, and that's the point of this exercise. Understanding the profound impact of visuals is crucial to benefiting from your vision and mission board to the fullest. It is your daily visual dose of inspiration, so remember to keep it within sight!

CHAPTER SUMMARY

Congratulations on completing this transformative chapter! By now, your life should feel meticulously formulated, guided by the powerful principle of BE-DO-HAVE. Becoming the person reflected in your calendar, doing the necessary tasks tracked in your daily accountability, and achieving your ultimate goals. By constructing your GPS, and embracing the 5-3-1 framework, and creating your vision and mission board, you've invested profoundly in your future. As you stand on the brink of a remarkable year, armed with meticulous planning and alignment, remember: you're among the elite three percent who write down their goals. Your comprehensive plan is the first step in your journey to becoming a REAL Top Producer.

6 🔑 TAKEAWAYS

🔑 As Dale Carnegie said, "One hour of planning can save you ten hours of DOING." A well-thought-out plan is the cornerstone of your journey to success.

🔑 Writing down your goals becomes a powerful directive to your subconscious, offering enhanced focus, better time efficiency, and greater clarity on your path to success.

🔑 Start constructing your planning portfolio using the GPS framework—Goal, Priorities and Strategies.

🔑 Envision and achieve milestones using the 5-3-1 framework. Summarize your aspirations over five years, three years and one year, providing a clear roadmap to your extraordinary future.

🔑 Harness the power of visualization by creating a vision and mission board that illustrates and encapsulates your goals and dreams.

🔑 Head to my website for even more resources, such as how to build your retirement plan.

ARE YOU A **REAL** TOP PRODUCER?

Find out:

Get your RTP Rating now! Take the assessment
to find out if you are currently a REAL Top Producer,
and if not, what you're missing to get there:

chrischopite.com/REALTopProducer/Assessment

CHAPTER 3

MASTER YOUR TIME

"Things rarely get stuck because of lack of time. They get stuck because the doing of them has not been defined."

DAVID ALLEN

Author of *Getting Things Done: The Art of Stress-Free Productivity*

WELCOME TO a paradigm shift in the pursuit of freedom and success. As realtors, we often view time-blocking and a structured schedule as constraints, fearing it may restrict the very freedom we entered this industry to enjoy. The irony lies in the realization that true freedom isn't granted. It's earned. In our search for autonomy, we must recognize that the ability to shape our destiny in real estate comes with a price. We can either work minimal hours and struggle, or embrace the reality of putting in the hard yards—fifty to seventy hours a week—to reap the amazing rewards this industry offers. Planning is key. We all have the same twenty-four hours; what we do with them determines our success. So, let's redefine the paradigm, break free from the notion that structure hinders, and instead let planning propel us toward the coveted title of Top Producer. Seizing control of our time is a critical step in this journey.

The freedom of a schedule

Here's a wild idea: true freedom is created by a well-structured schedule. What? Let me explain...

When every minute is accounted for, the burden of constant decision-making is lifted. You don't ever need to think or wonder or worry about what you should be doing. It's all there in black and white. This is not about the freedom to be idle, but the tranquility of an uncluttered mind. You will be free from questioning whether you're on track, diligently executing the strategies crucial for achieving daily priorities and, ultimately, whether you're steering toward the grand goal you set for yourself. The tighter your schedule, the lighter the mental load! For many, this mental peace is true freedom. A detailed, well put together schedule is key to the liberation of your mind. Your actions will align seamlessly with your aspirations without you having to even think about it. And all this, in turn, gives you the freedom to indulge in your off-time without the weight of work priorities invading your thoughts.

BOOK BONUS: I had a one-on-one interview with Jay Papasan, someone I admire as an author and business leader, in which we discussed the importance of mastering your time. Go to chrischopite.com/RTP and you will find it under resources. Jay Papasan is bestselling author, executive, business leader, and corporate speaker; you don't want to miss this audio!

Now let's get into how you can create a tighter than tight schedule...

Time-blocking—your secret weapon

As discussed in the last chapter, everyone needs to have non-negotiables; one of mine is my daily fitness routine—an unwavering commitment to my well-being that shapes each day of my life. Another is taking scheduled breaks. Every November, I plan my vacations for the upcoming year. These moments of relaxation are not left to chance; they are scheduled into my calendar. This proactive approach allows me to harmonize these breaks with the rest of my annual plans.

Let's unpack this further by dissecting my work year— a program created with intention and dedication—to help you get a sense of how your life as a striving Top Producer might look:

- Forty-eight weeks dedicated to business

- Four weeks reserved for vacation or personal time

- Sundays are sacred personal days, when I spend quality moments with my children, complete household tasks, and connect with friends and family. I also do my weekly planning.

For a Top Producer, Monday to Saturday is a sanctuary for business. The commitment to these six days is unwavering, and the only retreat from this intensive schedule comes with the strategic move of "recapturing your time." This involves delegating tasks to talented individuals who can seamlessly replace your responsibilities (more about this in Chapter 9). Until then, as a Top Producer, you get things done—it's the essence of our commitment.

Beyond the work year, I also allocate time for critical daily and weekly non-negotiables—items that are hard-wired into the calendar and cannot be moved for any reason. These include:

- Team meetings

- Wellness blocks that make time for meals, movement, and other health-related activities

- Family time

- Essential sleep (six to seven hours a night)

There are many benefits to time-blocking. It ensures that lead generation, crucial conversations and booked appointments take precedence over less important activities. Critical tasks are prioritized and completed because they are allocated in the daily schedule. There is no room to hide. Time-blocking creates greater awareness of how well you are using your time. When you fall behind, you are prompted to adjust and realign. The core blocks act as pillars that ensure your professional and personal survival. Without planning your day by using time-blocking, you jeopardize your business and livelihood

How to time block

Begin with the broad strokes—label your blocks with generic terms like "work time." Gradually refine this approach by using colours and adding the finer details. Envision your day and foresee its effectiveness each morning.

The objective is to let your calendar govern your actions. If an unexpected urgent matter arises, you stand firm, anchored by your big goal and fuelled by your big WHY. Suppose the task doesn't align with your overarching purpose. In that case, your initial response is resolute, "I'm not available at this time." Offer alternative slots, staying committed to your priority.

Remember: If it's not in your calendar, it doesn't exist. Even my wife, Raquel, finds her place in this digital network. Anything requiring my attention must be locked into the calendar; otherwise, it risks fading into the day's chaos.

Embrace technology

In effective time management, your digital ally is your calendar. At the forefront stands Google Calendar, a beacon of organization in the sea of schedules. But it doesn't matter whether you align with Google, Microsoft, or Apple; each platform offers a free version of their calendar application— the key to unlocking the potential of organized, purposeful days, months and years. Time-blocking without a structured calendar is akin to sailing without a compass; you risk drifting aimlessly. There is just one cardinal rule: USE ONE.

Technology is our steadfast companion, a tool for taming the chaos of schedules. Here's your toolkit:

- Google Calendar

- Project Management Software

- Task Manager

- In the Keller Williams World, Command—but, any client relationship management (CRM) system.

Embracing time-management technology gives you command over your time. It provides you with a perpetual reference point to keep you on track. Technological aids amplify efficiency and give you confidence as you navigate your day and close business deals with assurance.

When you ignore the wonderful technology available to help you master your time, you run several risks. You'll experience the discomfort of feeling lost. You may succumb to throwing your time away on unimportant tasks. You may misuse your time—your precious hours are not a playground and the consequences of not dedicating them to work will be damaging.

There are five clear steps to embedding technology into your time management:

1 Choose your calendar tool and master its features.

2 Explore diverse time control methods and AVOID multitasking!

3 Leverage the reminders on your phone.

4 Let automatic emails and notifications serve as your digital allies.

5 Sync your computer and phone for effortless productivity.

In a world inundated with distractions, let technology be your guide, steering you toward organized efficiency. Embrace your calendar, wield your digital arsenal, and let the symphony of controlled time elevate you to unparalleled confidence and success. Your time is a precious currency—spend it wisely.

The planning day— creating an eight-day week

In my routine, Sundays are sacred for both planning my work week and family bonding. The planning comes first. I use Sunday mornings, before the family wakes up, to set the stage for the coming week. The day kick starts at 4:45 a.m., and by 5:00 a.m. I'm immersed in preparing for the week ahead. Sunday mornings are dedicated to strategic planning, email clearing, content creation, and organizing computer files—essentially addressing tasks that often escape my attention during the week. I recommend you do this too. The key is to plan comprehensively, ensuring every facet of your upcoming week is considered.

Don't fall into the trap of NEVER thinking about work on a Sunday. The risk of maintaining excessive distance from your work-life on Sunday is that Monday then becomes a day of frantic preparation. Juggling everyone's demands while attempting to fix problems makes it challenging to regain control of your week. The antidote lies in meticulous Sunday planning, ensuring a smooth and empowered start to each week. No more arriving at the office first thing Monday only to find you need to spend half the day organizing the coming week. Instead, you can hit the ground running.

This proactive approach transforms Mondays into Tuesdays—effectively giving you another day to seize when you can get stuff done. Approaching the week with confidence, conviction, and unyielding drive becomes the norm.

To implement this effectively:

- Allocate thirty to ninety minutes on Sunday to review the coming week.

- Use this time to assess family responsibilities.

- Cross-reference personal and business commitments.

- Initiate proposed changes to the schedule promptly—avoid last-minute adjustments.

Chunkification

As you endeavour to create a tight, seamless, non-negotiable schedule, it will be helpful to break down your tasks and goals from large, unwieldy and daunting to small and more manageable. That is—into smaller and smaller chunks. This way you'll be less likely to feel overwhelmed and can set the pace of progress to something that suits you. As you continue in your journey to becoming uber-organized, you can adapt and create an effective schedule and to-do list that is manageable for you and tailored to your individual needs and preferences.

It's a no-brainer, really. Breaking any process into steps makes it less overwhelming. If you throw yourself into the tiny details from the get-go, you may give up too easily. Diving into overly detailed planning can lead to analysis paralysis. Progressing at your own pace ensures that you're comfortable and in alignment with your unique schedule. It's important to be comfortable and pace yourself if you're going to stick it out for the long haul. Even if your initial schedule is incredibly basic, it's still better than having no schedule at all!

So how do we go about breaking down those mountains into molehills? Easy… do this:

- **Big Chunks**: Start with the broader strokes.

- **Smaller Tasks**: Transition to intermediate levels of detail.

- **Tiny details**: Dig into finer specifics gradually.

The key is to strike a balance, commencing with a broad overview and progressively incorporating more details over time. This approach ensures a sustainable and adaptable evolution toward a meticulously organized and effective schedule.

For example, lead generation is a BIG task, so how did I break it down? Like this:

- **Big Chunk**: Lead generation

- **Smaller Tasks**: Purchase 100 Google leads per month, making a total of 1,200 per year. Set this up so it happens automatically with a lead-generation company.

- **Tiny details**:

Afternoon lead generation 10:00 am—2:00 pm

Follow-ups 4:00—6:00 pm

Desired Daily Goal: 20 conversations

Weekly Goal: 100 conversations

Every Friday at 6:00 pm: Review lead-gen expenses and ensure we're on track for a 2% conversion rate on the year.

Which all adds up to a total of twenty-four transactions.

Once you adopt this process of chunkification, even the most daunting task will become manageable. The key, once you've chunkified your task, is to focus on the task at hand, forget about the scary big picture, and let the plan unfold. However, like everything, you'll have your moment to review the results. As noted above, in this particular example this happens every Friday at 6:00 pm.

CHAPTER SUMMARY

We've discovered that time-blocking is a crucial investment for mental freedom. Employing a digital application to organize your days and weeks provides a clear visual reference to assess whether past days are aligned with your goals and if current days are optimized for efficiency. Maintaining a tight schedule reduces wasted time and enables your team and significant other to synchronize their schedules with yours, facilitating the booking of personal or family time. It's a tool and habit too beneficial to ignore; incorporating it into your life yields remarkable results.

6 🗝️ TAKEAWAYS

🔑 Planning your time is the key to unlocking success in the real estate industry.

🔑 Blocking time for your most critical tasks is the best way to achieve the fastest results. Also, your commitment to working six days a week is a testament to the dedication required to thrive in this industry.

🔑 Embrace technology to control your schedules and follow a roadmap for increased efficiency and confidence.

🔑 True freedom emerges within a well-structured schedule. The tighter the schedule, the lighter the mental load, granting the freedom to enjoy off-time without work priorities looming.

🔑 Sunday is your strategic planning and family bonding day. By dedicating time to review the week, cross-reference commitments, and propose changes promptly, you will be guided toward a smooth and empowered start each week.

🔑 Breaking large tasks into small ones will prevent them from feeling overwhelming and ensure they are completed.

ARE YOU A **REAL** TOP PRODUCER?

Find out:

Get your RTP Rating now! Take the assessment
to find out if you are currently a REAL Top Producer,
and if not, what you're missing to get there:

chrischopite.com/REALTopProducer/Assessment

PART TWO

CREATION

MASTER YOUR BRAND, PRESENCE & MARKETING

HERE'S A **REAL** STORY...

I was SUPER nervous; it was my first listing appointment from the online lead-generation campaign I was running. I had started working with a company that was providing online leads, and it was expensive, but I had accepted that the way I was going to build my business was by generating online leads.

Well, it was time. I remember them like it was yesterday—they were amazing people, Jackie and Benny—and they had NO CLUE that they were my first official listing appointment from this new business campaign. The listing was a $1.2 million detached home and the purchase was a $1.1 million detached house in Vaughan, Ontario. Here's how I got the listing and helped them buy a house.

I donned a smart suit and tie, and walked into the office. I vacuumed the carpet, I spritzed some nice air freshener, I put on some jazz, and I switched on the TV on the wall, which said, "Welcome Benny and Jackie." When they arrived, I offered them water, asked them how the drive was, thanked them for coming to see me, and off we went with the presentation.

I had spent all night working on a highly personalized presentation. There were pictures of their house; statistics about the community they lived in, including details about who purchases in that community; examples of the videos I had made in the past; print marketing material I had from previous listings that they could examine; examples of my newspaper ads; and images of my CRM and database of potential clients who might buy their home.

The presentation was branded with my logo, my colours and my essence.

Benny was an executive in his company, well versed, professional—but quiet. Jackie asked most of the questions. But mid-way through the presentation, Benny interrupted to ask, "You did ALL THIS for us?... Wow, I'm impressed."

When the presentation was over, they signed the listing agreement at a full five percent commission; EIGHT MONTHS in advance. It was unheard of. Because of this I was able to really plan out the marketing campaign around their listing, take our time looking for their new home, and really provide exceptional value to them.

This story is an example of what happens when Branding, Presence and Marketing come together, and it's an absolute game-changer for the REAL Top producer. Quality matters.

The energy in the room, in my voice, in the way I dressed left them NO reason to say, "I don't trust him." Everywhere they looked they saw PROfessionalism.

It was a memorable listing presentation. I'll always remember Benny and Jackie, and I'll always be grateful to them for taking a chance on me.

Welcome to the pivotal concept that defines your journey to becoming a REAL Top Producer. Here's the big idea—you ready? Until you've built your brand, perfected your presence and mastered your marketing, you are not a REAL Top Producer. In Part 2 we're going to learn about increasing your BPM—your brand, presence and marketing. In musical terms this stands for beats per minute. And this is what you need to do for your business—up the tempo, increase the energy, and make yourself stand out and beat at a higher energy level than your competition.

CHAPTER 4

BRANDING &
THE BUSINESS

"The best companies in the world don't sell—they brand.
For example, Apple never tried to 'convert' you into
buying an iPhone. Instead, they paint a picture of the 'iPhone
experience.' They focus on branding. I do the same."

GARY VAYNERCHUK
Serial entrepreneur, Chairman of VaynerX,
CEO of VaynerMedia and five-time
New York Times bestselling author

BEING A REAL Top Producer is NOT just about money. It's about longevity and standing out in your industry as a force to be reckoned with. Success in real estate isn't just a stroke of luck. It comes about through hard work, meticulous planning and unwavering commitment. Being a REAL Top Producer IS about becoming a name that resonates in every conversation. Think of the Frank Leos and Sam McDaddis in Canada—those whose brands are household names.

A crucial step to becoming a household name is nailing your branding. Branding isn't a mere formality; it's a critical step in building your business. It's the key to unlocking trust, and a well-crafted brand pays dividends far beyond the initial investment. A robust brand can be the catalyst for the life you've envisioned.

Creating a real estate brand requires you to undertake thoughtful exercises to understand your audience. Know your ideal clients intimately, tailor your brand to their needs, infuse it with your unique vibe, and witness the birth of a powerful business brand.

Let's not just learn; let's start crafting the brand that will set you apart. The playfield is yours.

Look beyond the licence

So, there I am, I have a real estate license... Good for me. When I look back to the day I got my license, I wish I would have known how much hard work was in front of me. Not that all those tests weren't nerve wracking and stressful, but the reality is that the moment you get your license is the moment you realize that playtime is over and now you have to go and actually work. But here's the catch—you don't really know how to. Because you have NO IDEA how to GET the business! The first step, of course, is developing your brand.

A CAUTIONARY NOTE: Branding is something you work on outside your lead-generation hours. You do not want to be building your brand and designing your business cards when you should be adding people to your database and/or having conversations with prospects!

A real estate license is a start, but a powerful brand does the heavy lifting for future success. Don't be afraid to invest in your brand. Stop the paradox of wanting millions while spending nothing. Understand that Top Producers invest. Successful realtors grasp the need to invest in their brand because spending money and time to build a brand yield returns far beyond mere hustling.

Invest now to secure a future where your brand attracts business effortlessly. Embark on this journey to create a brand that represents you and becomes a timeless legacy that resonates with your audience. Start the process now, investing wisely for a prosperous future. Here are some ways to gather inspiration for your brand:

- Explore Google, Indigo and magazines for inspiration.

- Tap into your family history for a brand with depth and legacy.

- Look into your personality to make it authentic.

- Research your target market to understand what will capture their attention.

You may want to hire professional help with your branding. When looking for the right people to hire, there are a few things to keep in mind. You really need a company and people who will be patient with you. Branding should not be rushed. If their main concern right off the bat is finances and timelines, they are surely the wrong people to be working with you. Timelines and finances are secondary when building a brand.

Whomever you hire needs to know that whatever the final branding is, it needs to inspire you—it should make you want to show off, represent and build that brand. The team you hire will have a process, but ensure you explain to them that they need to understand that you're looking for something that will MOVE you, which is likely to require more than some of your favourite colours and a bunch of AI generated logos slapped together.

Remember—creativity, inspiration and impact must be at the forefront of your branding conversation.

Get the logo right

Creating your logo is a critical step in creating your brand. It is more than an emblem; it reflects who you are. When designing it, keep these principles in mind:

- Don't get too fancy.

- Opt for a design that aligns with your values.

- Choose symbolism that resonates with your target audience.

- Keep it strictly to the point.

- Recognize that complexity in design will yield more hurdles when working on stationery and print; keep it "clean."

Unlike opening a franchise with hefty initial costs, you don't need to break the bank for an effective logo. When I started, I took some time to envision and plan what my brand should be, look like, say and represent. What exactly did I stand for? I started to work with a graphic designer and slowly built out what a graphic representation of who I am should look like. Let's have a look at my original logo so I can explain the WHY around it.

I wanted my branding to be clean, not noisy. I wanted people to see my colours, logo and myself as a person and feel confident that I knew what I was doing. Every tiny aspect of this logo is there for a reason:

- The key in the middle means "Let's unlock the world of real estate," and also "Let me take you home; let's find the key to this 'home' you seek."

- The circular shape represents a door knob—on a door that I want to help you open.

SYMBOL CONSTRUCTION

LOGO CONSTRUCTION

IDENTITY

FIGURE 4.1 Chris's logo

- The colour (which you can't see in the book) is maroon, or "Vinotinto" in Spanish—the national colour of Venezuela, where I was born.

- There's clearly a C in it, which stands for both my first and my last name.

- The whole logo is clean and tidy, to emit a feeling of seriousness, commitment, and good organization. The font spelling out my name is also clean and professional.

It took me some time to nail the design for the logo, but I devoted time at night or early in the morning, when my clients and the rest of the world was sleeping, to review it, sit with it, think about how others would see it, what it represented and ensure I got it right.

Don't be afraid to hire help if needed. When considering hiring a designer, providing clear direction and articulating your vision is crucial. Avoid vague requests, as providing detailed outlines will significantly assist designers in delivering precisely what you desire. To streamline communication and ensure efficiency, utilize the logo questionnaire available at chrischopite.com/RTP. This downloadable tool is a valuable resource, saving time and money in the design process.

Create a stationery package

When building a brand, key materials such as business cards, folders, and promotional materials influence how you show up to listing presentations and client meetings. These things are important, as they show just how detail oriented you are and establish your business as a top contender. They are also a crucial element in sending the right message about your brand.

Having a clear vision, which informs how you share your story and embodies your values, far outweighs the cost associated with these materials. Even creating a digital version allows you to revisit and reinforce the image of your future prominent brand. It serves as a powerful reminder that you are not just in this business for short-term gains; you are committed to going all-in, aiming to eventually become a REAL Top Producer.

The stationery package will ensure that anyone you hire to print material for you has a document that they can refer to so that all your branding is uniform. Your stationery package is the ONE TRUTH about your brand. Whomever you're going to use for all your merchandise and printed material will know how to design, what fonts, colors and design elements to use when designing and finalizing any material for you.

Use social media to tell your story

Next up in the journey to creating a strong brand is leveraging social media for all it's worth. Use all the social media within your reach to tell your story and win the mindshare battle. The great thing about social media is that it gives you a chance to craft who you are. It's invaluable for consolidating your brand and ensuring people know who you are and what you represent. Make sure your brand is the one people think of when they need a real estate professional. Use social media to connect with your clients, ask for referrals, get those Google reviews—make it a habit to post and stay relevant. You MUST get comfortable in front of the camera; for Top Producers, this is one of the activities that you must track and a habit you must build out.

Here's a 101 on getting started...

The 5Ps of social media
Leveraging social media requires a robust strategic approach, which is encapsulated by the five Ps:

1. Planning—content calendar
Embark on your social media journey with meticulous planning. Develop a detailed content calendar that serves as your roadmap. Outline the topics, themes, and key messages you want to convey. This planning phase gives structure to your content and ensures a consistent and purposeful presence on social platforms.

Go to chrischopite.com/RTP to download a content calendar you can use to prepare your entire month of content and captions.

2. Preparation—practice
Many people assume that creating content is as easy as turning on a camera and pressing record. You would be surprised how much time Top Producers and influencers spend on writing and scripting what they will say on camera. Before stepping into the spotlight of social media, hone your skills through practice. Familiarize yourself with the nuances of each platform, experiment with content formats, and refine your delivery. This preparation phase builds confidence and expertise, laying the foundation for compelling and engaging content that puts your brand front and centre.

3. Profile—all profiles MUST be aligned and put together
Your social media profiles are the digital reflection of your brand. Ensure uniformity and coherence across all platforms. From profile pictures to bios, maintain consistency in visuals and messaging. A well put together profile establishes

credibility and makes it easier for your audience to recognize and connect with your brand.

Ensure that links and calls to action are included in all your social media bios. A strong call to action/slogan can help move your followers into taking the next step. Providing that link to where you want them to go allows for more opportunities to either build more rapport or book more appointments.

4. Presence—speak to your audience

Establishing a meaningful presence involves more than just posting content. Engage with your audience by responding to comments, initiating conversations, and addressing queries. Just a small like on a comment can strengthen the connection between you and your followers. A comment response is a step above that and featuring that comment is even better. Understand your audience's preferences and tailor your content to resonate with them. Building a genuine and interactive presence fosters a community around your brand.

5. Performance—put on a show

Elevate your social media game by treating it as a performance. Create content that captivates and entertains your audience. Utilize storytelling techniques, incorporate visuals, and leverage the unique features of each platform. A well-thought-out performance captures attention and contributes to the memorable and shareable nature of your content. A consistent performance that captures the essence of your brand will make that brand stronger and stronger.

Now let's take a quick look at the content of your content.

The three pillars of content

When crafting your content, make sure it embodies three key attributes:

1 **Professional**: Maintain a polished and professional demeanour across all content. High-quality visuals and well-crafted messaging reinforce your brand's professionalism, while bad or shaky camera work, poor audio and an unnatural communication style will make you look unprofessional. I am NOT saying that you need to be in a suit and a wedding gown every time... but I am saying that you should be heard clearly and mind your lighting. This is the one thing that can make a MASSIVE difference—*light is to a camera lens what water is to a fish!*

2 **Educational**: Position yourself as an industry authority by sharing valuable insights, tips and knowledge. Educational content not only adds value for your audience but also establishes your expertise. And it goes beyond real estate news and updates. Aim to be the go-to person for all news in your target area and establish your presence as a public figure.

3 **Entertaining**: Inject an element of entertainment into your content. Whether through humour, storytelling, or engaging visuals, entertaining content enhances audience engagement and leaves a lasting impression. Editing is important here. Ensure that you present the best parts of your brand and avoid the feeling of creating content for the sake of creating content. Capturing the attention of your viewers will give you the opportunity to engage them and turn that attention into business with various offers and calls to action (CTAS).

Mastering the 5 Ps of social media requires a strategic blend of planning, preparation, profile curation, active presence and performance. These elements must also align with three content pillars to ensure a compelling social media strategy.

CHAPTER SUMMARY

Your brand is everywhere—from your logo to the content of your socials. It's a reflection of your business. It's the way people see you and how they see you is how they perceive you. Your brand needs to be clear, reflect your values and who you are, but also speak to your audience in a language they understand and respond to. It's the first step in building genuine connection and rapport. And it is ever evolving. You will change as your business grows, and so you must consistently check that your branding is directly reflective of who you are, the services you offer, and what people can expect from you.

6 🔑 TAKEAWAYS

🔑 Your brand represents what your clients can expect.

🔑 Build your brand when the world sleeps, not in Lead-Gen Time!

🔑 Hire the help you need—it can save you a ton of time.

🔑 Ensure your logo means something to you AND your potential clients.

🔑 Make the effort to create a stationery package, even if it's just a digital package—it's the perfect canvas for your branding.

🔑 Leverage social media to get your brand out there.

ARE YOU A **REAL** TOP PRODUCER?

Find out:

Get your RTP Rating now! Take the assessment to find out
if you are currently a REAL Top Producer, and if not, what
you're missing to get there:

chrischopite.com/REALTopProducer/Assessment

CHAPTER 5

PRESENCE & PROFESSIONALISM

"If you look good, you feel good;
if you feel good, you play good;
if you play good, they pay good."

DEION "PRIME TIME" SANDERS
American football coach and former two-
sport star player in the National Football
League and Major League Baseball

IN THIS chapter we will get into the energy aspect of being a Top Producer. You see, there's a confidence that you must possess, a lot of which comes from absorbing and applying the advice from the previous chapters. But there is no REAL Top Producer without the presence that comes from being PROfessional. That is, showing up at your best—well groomed and well appointed.

Part of this is having a solid understanding of being in the moment—of being present and prepared, *always* prepared, to deliver. Yes, half the battle is won by showing up, but you can win 100% of the battles if you show up confident, prepared and ready to transfer positive energy toward your goal.

Be PRO-fessional

Defining what makes a professional goes beyond expertise, accumulated hours and pay scale. While credentials and experience contribute to professionalism, we need to go deeper to discover what makes someone truly professional.

Even an individual with ten years of law school, a decade of work experience and a substantial 100,000 hours devoted to their craft may fall short of being a true professional. If, despite their impressive and extensive background, they consistently arrive late to meetings, exhibit disorganization in their workspace, and showcase a tendency to fabricate information when faced with uncertainty, their professionalism comes into question. Mere longevity and experience do not define a professional. Our professional roles should be underpinned by certain core values.

The essence of professionalism lies in embracing fundamental values that extend beyond qualifications. It involves embodying punctuality, resourcefulness and organization— traits that build trust, establish a reliable reputation, and foster a conducive work environment. In this context, professionalism is not merely about what you know, but how you integrate knowledge, respect and efficiency into your daily actions. I like to define professionalism through three fundamental attributes: punctuality, resourcefulness and organization.

Let's take a closer look at those...

Punctuality

In the professional realm, reliability is paramount. A top-producing professional embodies punctuality. This begins with a commitment to showing up on time, as promised. Trust is the bedrock of any professional relationship with clients, team members, or business associates. When you say you'll call me back, or you'll be there at 4:00 pm—do it. It's that simple. Just do what you say you're going to do. A professional understands the weight of their word and feels a profound responsibility to deliver on their promises.

Yes, things go wrong, and when they do, you better be sure you communicate the situation, keep the other party up to date, and offer a lot of apologies for disrespecting their time. Treat others as you want to be treated; If you don't like waiting fifteen minutes for other people to arrive, don't make *them* wait fifteen minutes for *you* to arrive.

Top Producers arrive early, they set up, and they welcome people as they arrive. They become a red carpet for their guests, clients and other professionals they work with. I want you to make your clients feel special—give them the impression that you can't wait to get to see them. So be early, or at the very least, be on time.

Resourcefulness

We're living in an era inundated with information, which is coming at a speed we simply cannot keep up with. Therefore, the true professional knows that his service and his resources are critical. A true professional curates an extensive network, including advisory teams, consultants, and subject experts. The ability to tap into these resources distinguishes a professional from the rank amateur and earns admiration and respect. Providing accurate and expert advice becomes a significant advantage in a world where connections can be more important than individual knowledge.

As a Top Producer, you can be a resource machine for your team and clients. When someone asks, "And how do the zoning bylaws affect the purchase of this property?" a true professional says: "I'm glad you asked. Let me chat with Eric West from the City of Toronto's permit department, and I'll have that information over to you by the end of this week." BANG! That's being a professional. You don't need to know everything; you just need to build your resources and create a vast network to guide clients and contribute to their business endeavours.

Here's where you have a chance to really show the extent of your impact, your network and how lucky your clients and your colleagues are to have you in their lives—when you can pull a critical resource out at the drop of a hat, you suddenly become VITAL to any meeting, any opportunity and any conversation.

Organization

The often overlooked yet essential aspect of professionalism is organization. Don't say you don't have time to be organized; make the time. Being organized will make you more efficient, calmer, and, more importantly, more likely to become a REAL Top Producer.

A forgotten art in today's fast-paced world, organization brings order to your personal and professional life. When your clients and team members see order—in the way you keep your desk, in the way you keep your computer's desktop, in the way you keep your car, in the way you dress—they see a true professional.

Organization and order are critical, and this extends to the way you communicate. How efficiently you structure your message is part of being organized. Organized means you know where things are, and you're able to explain the processes of things because your thoughts are organized.

Organization goes beyond the office and extends to your personal space and details like the way your shoes are kept at home. Every detail of a professional's life must be in order. If your life looks like it's in shambles, it probably is.

Many people try to get out of being organized by saying, "I live in organized chaos." You take a peek in their office and it looks like Tom and Jerry have been filming in there—stuff everywhere, piled on top of everything—it's a mental breakdown waiting to happen. How can you be your best for your clients and your team members if you can't handle your own personal space?

From the tidiness of the desk to the structured layout of a message, a professional understands the significance of maintaining order. If you struggle with being organized, you may benefit from courses in this forgotten art.

Right, that's professionalism in a nutshell, now let's move on to another critical component of a REAL Top Producer's toolkit: the ability to be present.

Be present

Professionalism is easy to understand; it's a clear concept. What is harder to understand is the concept of presence; this is more subjective. But to be a REAL Top Producer, you must have the right presence. So, what is it? Let me demystify this.

Presence is:

- The state or fact of existing, occurring, or being present in a place or thing

- A person or thing that exists or is present in a place but is not seen

From this dictionary definition, we can conclude that presence is about BEING THERE. And after all, they say that showing up is half the battle. But what about the quality and strength of your presence? What sort of energy do you emit? Is it strong and charismatic? Clear and confident? Your presence will show in the way you speak, your confidence, your knowledge, how organized and prepared you are—these are all elements of presence. Your tone, the speed of your discussions, your level of interest in a person are also indicators of your presence. The key is to get these things right so that your presence is magnetic.

When your energy is good, and you show up with bigger guns, a better strategy, better prepared, better trained, and with more experience, your chances of winning the battle are close to a guaranteed win. It's important to work on your presence *before* you charge into battle. Top Producers don't show up unprepared. By now you might be wondering, "Chris, how do I work on my presence?"

The first step is to work on your appearance.

Look good to feel good

Appearances matter—it's a mantra that Top Producers live by. Looking good isn't just about vanity; it's a strategic choice that is critical to career success. Top Producers understand the impact of their presence—whether people are engaging with them in person, through pictures, or on video—and they recognize that potential clients are always observing, often when least expected. Dressing for the role you aspire to, not the one you currently occupy, is a principle you must adhere to.

Allocate time for self-care, seek professional advice on styling if needed, and be aware of fashion trends. Always present yourself as if you're applying for your dream job. REAL Top Producers embody professionalism and amplify their presence through their appearance, but don't worry—this doesn't mean splurging $5,000 a month on wardrobe or salon visits—the emphasis is on paying attention to attire and gauging the message it conveys.

Confidence, not cockiness, should exude from your outfit. Demonstrating your respect for clients' time by putting effort into your appearance sends a powerful message. One of my mentors, Harold Persad, taught me always to wear a suit and tie to gain trust. While perceptions of suits and ties may have evolved, there's still merit in dressing appropriately.

The key is to dress for the occasion. If you find yourself overdressed, match the energy of your client to avoid creating discomfort. Being a well-dressed professional isn't a drawback; you can offset its impact by radiating upbeat energy. This approach ensures that your attire complements your identity as a highly knowledgeable, resourceful and pleasant individual—a truly impactful combination.

Looking good goes beyond mere professionalism and influences your energy. When you look good, you feel good. And when you feel good, you do good. Being careful and conscientious about your appearance will ignite a strong and charismatic energy within you, which will enhance and strengthen your presence.

Level up your presence

Consider two agents. One has been doing between six and eight deals a year for the last five years. The other is a Top Producer who does between thirty-six and forty-eight deals a year and seems to be living the life. What is that successful agent doing differently with his presence? How do you level up like him? Here are some key strategies he is likely to be employing:

- **Know your market**: Make sure you know your niche market inside out—this will give you confidence.

- **Practice regularly**: This will also boost your confidence. Don't skip role-playing and scripting; dress rehearsals mean that when you present you will be polished and powerful.

- **Educate yourself**: Learn more about your industry, improve your jargon, attend seminars, and work on your speaking skills. Again, this will give you greater confidence.

- **Know that you're being judged**: You might not like it, but it's a reality. When prospective clients are sizing you up, they are judging you—so get over it. Being resentful or feeling like this is unfair will only undermine your presence. Worry about more important things; this is business, and they get to choose you. To that end, give people NO reason to judge you unfairly—don't, for example, come to a presentation straight after a workout without showering first.

- **Remember that you're being watched**: There are cameras everywhere—on your phone, your computer, at traffic lights—and they're all watching you. You're never alone. You are always present, so make sure you have the RIGHT presence. Do your best, be your best, and do the right thing—always. If you're always doing your best and always doing the right thing, life is easier and simpler. You don't have to check yourself to see if you're presentable, you never have to lie to cover something up. People sense that and will want to work with you; you instill trust with your mere presence.

I'm going to finish off this chapter with one more idea for strengthening your presence. Now, this is a bit "out there," but hear me out. I want you to think of your presence as an output of energy. Take a moment and visualize your presence as a halo around your body. Now, take this halo with you everywhere you go. Your job is to ensure your halo is bright and strong and your presence is unmistakable. You can revisit this little thought exercise any time you feel your presence weakening—think of that halo, and lean into it at critical times, like before a big presentation. If you're skeptical, at least give it a try. And remember, nobody but you need know that you have this halo, this forcefield that you're envisioning.

Always ask yourself: Do you emit trust? People do business with those they like and trust, but trust is more important than likability. Many people may love you, but if they don't trust you because your "presence" is sending the wrong message, they won't hire you as their agent.

CHAPTER SUMMARY

Sales is a transfer of energy—people only want GREAT energy around them and we know that people ONLY do business with people they like and trust. When we show up PROfessionally and have a strong, positive presence, we emit the energy we need to obtain the results we want. Got it?

Professionalism is straightforward—be punctual, resourceful and organized. Presence is more subjective, but no less important. The way you dress and speak, your confidence, your knowledge, your tone, your level of interest IN the person—these are all elements of your presence. When you get these right, you will have immense magnetism and effortlessly attract business.

6 ⊙━⇒ TAKEAWAYS

⌂ Being PRO-fessional means being punctual, resourceful and organized.

⌂ Your appearance is important. Clients WILL judge a book by its cover, so make sure you look good.

⌂ Presence is not about an expensive wardrobe, it is HOW you WEAR your wardrobe.

⌂ Looking good has the added bonus of making you feel good, which in turn will boost your energy.

⌂ Sales is a transfer of energy, so be positive, outgoing and energetic.

⌂ Uplift your energy by taking a moment to go inwards and imagine your energy as a halo around your body, then take that energy into the room with you.

ARE YOU A **REAL** TOP PRODUCER?

Find out:
Get your RTP Rating now! Take the assessment to find out if you are currently a REAL Top Producer, and if not, what you're missing to get there:

chrischopite.com/REALTopProducer/Assessment

CHAPTER 6

MARKETING & MESSAGING

"The goal of marketing is to create a customer who is so loyal, they will never consider buying from anyone else."

WALT DISNEY
Renowned American animator, film
producer and entrepreneur and co-founder
of The Walt Disney Company

OH MARKETING! It's a term thrown around just as much as "Top Producer." People are often puzzled by it—what exactly is marketing, and why is it so important?

Let's make it simple: marketing attracts—it's the worm—and sales is the hook... Get it?

Welcome to one of the most important chapters of our journey. This is where you'll learn the art of attracting people to your business rather than the conventional approach of chasing after them. How good does that sound? Imagine the satisfaction of having individuals seek you out for business. But this doesn't happen magically; it demands dedicated time, effort, and, yes, investment.

Decode the mystery of marketing

Okay, let's unpack that definition of marketing a bit further. There is often confusion about when marketing becomes sales. Different businesses may wield different strategies, but a Top Producer seeking clarity needs to understand precisely when this crucial transfer occurs. As you can see from my cute drawing below, it's a bit of a grey area. Marketing is everything that leads to the first conversation you have with a client. Sales is everything that happens from the first conversation onwards and how you serve your client—all the way to the point at which the transaction takes place. Again—anything that happens before the person knows you is marketing; once you're talking to them, you're up; that's when you become the salesperson, or, as a REAL Top Producer thinks of it, the client educator.

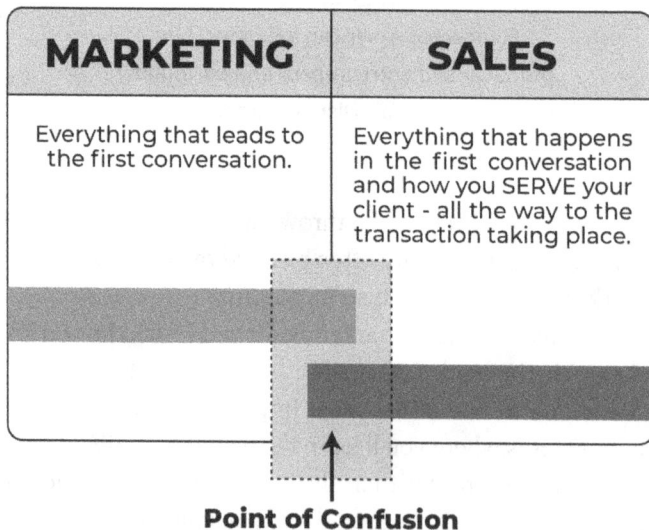

MARKETING	SALES
Everything that leads to the first conversation.	Everything that happens in the first conversation and how you SERVE your client - all the way to the transaction taking place.

Point of Confusion

FIGURE 6.1 Marketing to sales

Like I said before: marketing is the BAIT, sales is the HOOK!

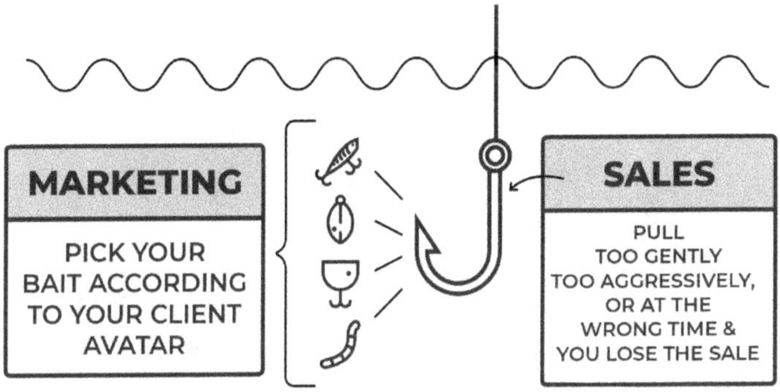

FIGURE 6.2 The bait and hook

I hope that's really clear now, because I'm about to complicate things.

REAL Top Producers understand there are two marketing funnels in their real estate business. One is about selling our service, and the other is about selling the product—that is, real estate. And if you want to sell real estate, you first have to sell your service.

Here's a graphic to help you understand...

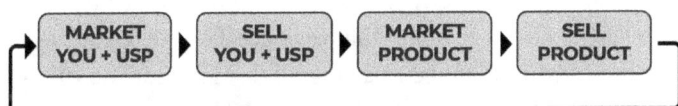

FIGURE 6.3 How real estate professionals do marketing

This one illustrates how the process repeats. You market your service—that is, yourself and your USP (Unique Selling Proposition)—then you sell your service, then you market your product—that is, the property you're selling on behalf of the client you've just sold your service to—then you sell the property. Then rinse and repeat. Market your service, sell your service, market your product, sell your product, market your service, sell your service, market your product, and on and on it goes.

The point I am trying to make here is that marketing is a permanent feature of your business. A REAL Top Producer understands this, and doesn't let up just because he's bagged a prestigious client or sold an ultra-expensive listing.

Okay, so, if you're going to be doing a lot of marketing, we better take a closer look at exactly what's involved.

Align your marketing

Marketing, especially GREAT marketing, can only take place when you know yourself, your product, and your message. In Part 1 you set your goals and learned how to build your plan. This was important, because in creating those goals and plans you get to know who you are and what you enjoy, and out of that you're going to pull all the information you need to build your marketing plan—also known as your messaging.

The first step in aligning your marketing is building your brand, which you read about in Chapter 4. The next step is knowing who your perfect and aspirational clients are. REAL Top Producers understand that they can't speak to everyone, but they can yell, dance and sing all day long for the RIGHT person—and that's enough for a bigger life than you imagined and enough to become and stay a REAL Top Producer for decades to come.

Consider this critical question: "Who do you serve?" Do some introspection and answer these three fundamental questions:

1 Who is your service directed toward?
2 What constitutes your niche market?
3 Where do your passions and aspirations lie?

It's important to be honest here. Find the answers from your inner convictions and passions, not from the last Instagram post you saw. You know how it is. You saw some other realtor saying that he made billions selling pre-construction, so now you also want to sell pre-construction. But are you being authentic, or just jumping on the bandwagon? If you want to sell pre-construction, go and research it, get to know the business well, and then, and only then, decide whether you want pre-construction to be your niche market. It can be extremely costly (mostly in your time) to enter a niche market without doing extensive research and finding out if you will enjoy the everyday struggles of that business approach. So do some research to assess whether it aligns with your business goals and, more importantly, if you will derive satisfaction from its day-to-day challenges.

Once you have nailed your niche—found exactly the right customer avatar and area of focus for your passions, strengths and aspirations—start putting out your message to the world. Your message should tell your niche customers what you do for them and should attract them to you. With a good message you will be able to attract the right people. And you need to keep on top of it. Top Producers are always working on their marketing messaging. Get eyes on your messaging—a REAL Top Producer must showcase themselves, their team and their company in a way that represents the clients they want to serve. The first impression is the ONLY impression.

Master the basics

Okay, so let's get down to business here. There's something you ought to know: some forms of marketing are free, and some require money to get them going. But all forms of marketing require you to give up one of two things—time or money. And in many cases, you will have to give away both time AND money.

Cost of Marketing		
Strategies	$	Time
FB Ads	✓	✓
Landing Pages	✓	✓
Website	✓	✓
SEO	✓	✓
Graphic Design	✓	✓
Email Campaigns	✓	✓
Stationery	✓	✓
Networking Events	✓	✓
Podcasts	✓	✓
Events	✓	✓
Guarantees	✓	✓
Community Engagements Campaigns	✓	✓

FIGURE **6.4** The time and money chart of marketing

One way to get some free marketing is to...

Partner up with vendors

You must have a list of vendor partners. These include mortgage brokers, home inspectors, window cleaners, stagers—anyone who has a role in real estate. If you don't have a list of vendor partners, then you really don't have a full grip on the process. Having these relationships can be critical for a real estate professional. And the really great thing is, you can partner up with them to market your business for free—or at least for just a little legwork. Here's how to go about it:

- Seek industry partners targeting the same audience as you.

- Propose an alliance where you put in the legwork, and they make other contributions, such as covering printing costs for flyers, etc.

- Tailor the arrangement to be mutually beneficial and financially viable for both parties—it can take many forms, just ensure it works for both of you.

- Ensure their return on investment is, ideally, four times the amount invested, and at least double the initial investment.

Follow the 7-11-4 rule

One marketing theory, known as the "Rule of 7s," states that a potential customer must encounter a message at least seven times before taking action. Another theory is known as the "7-11-4 Rule." This is based on research by Google, which indicates a buyer needs seven hours of interaction across eleven touchpoints in four different locations before making a purchase.

Examples of touchpoints include:

- Website visits
- Social media feeds
- Advertisements
- A visit to your office
- Events

Locations (or formats) where customers might interact with you include:

- Print
- Radio
- TV
- Social media

Here's a graphic to illustrate how this looks like in practice:

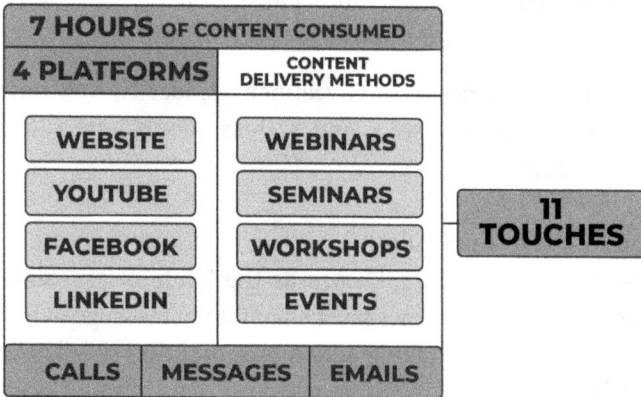

FIGURE 6.5 An example of the 7-11-4 rule

This marketing theory is all very well, but it represents AVERAGES. A REAL Top Producer will blast those averages out of the water. They will create a conversion in an average of five touches. A Top Producer knows what is trending in the world of marketing, and deploys these weapons. Furthermore, they are always on top of the results their marketing is yielding. By results I mean how many conversations are they getting from their marketing campaign. Because as you know, once you're talking to a prospect, you're selling.

Let's take a look at some of the techniques that REAL Top Producers deploy to make their marketing remarkable.

Make your marketing remarkable

Let's uncover a profound truth about marketing: EVERYTHING WORKS! The real game-changer? You. Your efforts will succeed provided you allocate sufficient time and find the right formula. Seek insights from seasoned mentors and coaches, or consider hiring a consultant to fast-track your journey. But remember, any marketing campaign requires both patience and consistency to flourish.

It's important to be patient, because if you're not you run the risk of dumping a marketing campaign that could have proved effective in the long run. These things take time to build. Remember how we talked about delaying gratification in Chapter 1? Well, this is the time to do that. Focus on the process and forget about results for the moment. Give things time to work. Have faith that your business is going in the right direction; don't be deceived by the apparent lack of results. It's not a lack of progress. Things are working; it's just not immediately apparent. Allow each campaign the time it needs. Compounded effort is a reality, leading to unexpected success. Pledge to the process, not just the results. Marry the journey; success will follow.

So, if everything works, how do you decide which methods to use? The short answer is: whatever fits your budget (money and time) and whatever you have the resources to pull off. And, most importantly, the one you're going to do CONSISTENTLY! To get you thinking, let's look at some of the elements that top-producing agents use to market themselves:

- **Professional branding**: Craft your business to be representative of a PROfessional. All your marketing material should be well branded and marked with your logo.

- **Online presence**: Create a user friendly and visually appealing website that showcases listings, services, and your expertise. Leverage social media platforms like Instagram, Facebook, X (formerlyTwitter) and LinkedIn to connect with potential clients and share relevant content.

- **High-quality photography and virtual tours**: Invest in professional photography and virtual tours for property listings to make them stand out online.

- **Email marketing**: Build and maintain a contacts database for email marketing campaigns. Regularly send out newsletters, market updates, and information about new listings.

- **Networking**: Attend local networking events, join professional associations, and collaborate with other real estate professionals to expand your network.

- **Client testimonials and reviews**: Showcase positive client testimonials and reviews on your website and marketing materials to build credibility.

- **Content marketing**: Create and share valuable content, such as blog posts, videos and infographics, to position yourself as an expert in the real estate industry.

- **Targeted advertising**: Use online advertising platforms like Google Ads and social media ads to target specific demographics and geographic areas.

- **Quality open houses**: Host well-promoted and professionally presented open houses to attract potential buyers and showcase properties.

- **Community involvement**: Get involved in the local community through sponsorships, charity events, and participation in community activities.

- **Stay informed about market trends**: Regularly update marketing materials and strategies based on changes in the real estate market.

- **Mobile optimization**: Ensure that all online platforms are optimized for mobile devices, as many people search for real estate on smartphones and tablets.

- **Use CRM (Customer Relationship Management) software**: Utilize CRM tools to manage client relationships, organize contacts, and streamline communication.

- **Continuous learning**: Stay informed about industry trends, new technologies, and best practices through ongoing education and professional development.

- **Specialization**: Consider specializing in a particular niche or type of real estate to differentiate yourself in the market.

By combining these strategies and adapting to changes in the real estate landscape, top-producing agents can effectively market themselves and their listings, ultimately attracting more clients and closing more deals. The key is to give it everything you've got, give it time so that you can determine exactly which strategies are producing results, then refine your marketing efforts until they're laser-focused on bringing the right customers straight to your door.

CHAPTER SUMMARY

REAL Top Producers understand their brand and their messaging, and they're able to create assets that send the right message to their intended client avatar. Top Producers have been able to pinpoint, often through trial and error, what's working and what isn't working. They put the effort in. Then they double down on what is working to secure the constant flow of attention in order to turn attention into sales calls and revenue.

6 TAKEAWAYS

- Marketing is what happens before you have that first conversation with a customer.

- Sales is everything that happens after you speak to a customer, right up to closing a deal.

- REAL Top Producers market both their services and the properties they sell.

- Your marketing must be targeted to your ideal customer, slotted into the right niche, and aligned with your personality and passions.

- All forms of marketing work. The secret is in hanging in there for the long haul, being patient and valuing process over results.

- When you identify a marketing hack that brings customers to your door, double down on it.

ARE YOU A **REAL** TOP PRODUCER?

Find out:

Get your RTP Rating now! Take the assessment to find out if you are currently a REAL Top Producer, and if not, what you're missing to get there:

chrischopite.com/REALTopProducer/Assessment

PART THREE

ELEVATION

TOOLS, TRACKING & TEAM

HERE'S A **REAL** STORY...

I was working non-stop two weeks straight; negotiating with buyers, selling a few properties. I was BUSY. What I thought was a "regular" ten-hour day turned into a sixteen-hour day. I was missing lunches, dinners, and time with my family.

Then one night I'm in my office, working—of course. It's 9:30 pm and suddenly I can't open my eyes and my head is pounding; something was seriously wrong. I barely made it to the car, but I managed to drive myself to the hospital... And I was there until 7:00 am the next day.

I was overly stressed, overworked, and on the brink of a massive collapse.

I decided at that moment that it was time to get some help. There are three ways to get immediate help in your business:

- Deploy systems and processes
- Adopt tools and technology
- Employ people

All three of these methods are important, but, and I say this from experience, the best and the most challenging way to grow is through people. Most REAL Top Producers, at the beginning of their career, suffered from a delusion that THEY can do it all better than anyone else. But this could not be further from the truth.

After my little "breakdown" and visit to the hospital, I sat down and asked myself some hard questions: Is this what success is supposed to feel like? Am I going to make it? Is this what I want for myself and my family? Is this the only way to build a successful real estate business? I didn't like the answers, and so it became my goal to work a little smarter and start to look for ways to grow my business that would not send me to the emergency room.

One thing I implemented right away was to start looking at my database, establish where most of my business came from, and get more purposeful around the clients I wanted to work with.

The second thing I did was become more vocal about wanting to grow a team. I started to look for my first hire— an administrative assistant who could help me keep the business I currently had and, more importantly, grow it to new heights.

I also looked around and audited whether the brokerage I was currently partnered with was the right fit for the goals I had in mind. The short answer was that I needed more support. So, I looked for a brokerage that offered more opportunities and support to grow a team. When I found one, I made that change so I could give myself every advantage possible.

Deciding I needed help was the best thing I ever did. As I write this today, Vaughan Real Estate Advisors (VREA) has grown to three agents, a transaction coordinator, and a marketing department, and the projection for growth is exponential. All this in the four years since I founded the company.

One of the reasons I have been able to attract excellent personnel is the care taken to craft a brand that stands out from the rest. The team has grown organically, with key personnel inspired to come on board by their massive belief in the values of the team and company. We have not attracted people who are ONLY interested in making a living—we have attracted people who want to help the business grow to new heights and, thus, make a GREAT living—*funny how that works!*

People naturally want to join the company because they see that this company stands out—there's something different about it, something special, the energy is right. This proves that focusing on increasing VREA's BPM—Branding, Presence and Marketing—was the right approach at the beginning. Trust the process.

In Part 3, we're going to ELEVATE your business—start looking at the essential practices and activities that will take you from a solid, steady business and set you on the road to becoming a REAL Top Producer; consistently. These include some of the more boring facets of business—taxes, accounting, finances, tracking your business, and so on—but believe me when I say they are game changers. And, perhaps most critically, we're going to look at how to grow your team.

CHAPTER 7

SYSTEMS AND PROCESSES

"People fail, but systems WIN!"

LES BROWN
Motivational speaker and author

WELCOME TO the wonderful world of sales mastery! In this chapter we cover two important topics: learning how to document your processes and getting a handle on the basics of accounting and taxes. While your journey to expertise and financial success is a solo venture, there comes a moment when you must transition from mere sales to methodical documentation.

In the most basic terms, sales is what you do—after all we are salespeople—but this is not the end piece: the sale begins a whole new world of greatness for you and your business. And just one sale is enough for you to start the right habits. ONE sale is enough for you to write down your processes. ONE sale is enough to create a system around how you would like your business to be run. The point I'm making is that you don't have to think that only people who do 100 transactions per year are allowed to have systems and processes. Start thinking like a REAL Top Producer, and turn your sales into leverageable tools that you can build your empire on.

It's time to bite the bullet, and hit the desk for some serious paperwork. You're going to construct your first operations manual and fill it with your standard operating procedures (SOPs) and proven processes tailored to yield results. Once your processes are outlined, you'll deploy systems that align seamlessly with these methodologies, ushering in a new era of operational efficiency.

This chapter guides you on when and how to initiate the development of your processes and systems.

Track your top tasks

Congratulations, you're in the thick of it—closing deals, listing homes, acquiring properties, and revelling in the influx of commissions. Your water-tight business model and diligent planning efforts are reaping rewards, and you're heading toward the zenith of your real estate enterprise.

Now, I won't get into the intricacies of selling here. You've undergone the necessary training and coaching, accumulating experience and honing your skills through relentless practice. Instead, I'll get into the systems and processes you should be focusing on.

Sounds boring, right? But if you take the plunge now, you'll save an abundance of time. By establishing your processes and systems promptly, you avoid the need to revisit and reconstruct your sales experiences. Seize the moment, embark on creating your processes and systems today— start now. Your future self will thank you.

Let's take a look at some key tasks that should be locked into your schedule and automated so that you barely have to think about them.

The following are crucial tasks that demand a real estate agent's unwavering attention:

1 **Lead Generation**: identify and cultivate leads to sustain a robust pipeline. Without leads you don't have a real estate business.

2 **Lead Follow-up**: maintain consistent communication with leads and clients, nurturing relationships in and out of your database for future opportunities.

3 **Appointments**: you must be going on appointments, if not daily, at least weekly. You must get in front of the clients who are willing and able to sign an agreement and secure you as their real estate consultant and confidante.

4 **Scripting and Role-playing**: master the art of effective communication through scripted dialogues and role-playing scenarios. Yes, you play how you practice, so make your practice intense and practice often.

At this juncture, your focus should be on excelling in these fundamental areas. Also, you need to integrate these tasks into your routine with precision. Executing these tasks seamlessly and confidently within your schedule, free from interruptions, will yield the highest and most rewarding results. If you do that, your real estate journey is on a trajectory of sustained success.

So, I bet you're asking yourself, "How in the world do I incorporate these things into my life? Into my schedule?" I can answer that question...

Lead generation starts by simply having conversations about real estate on a daily basis. Be purposeful on what your daily strategy will be. For example, walk out of your house with five business cards in your right pocket, and when you come home that day aim to have NO business cards in your right pocket and five business cards in your left pocket. The five in your left pocket should be from people that you did not know that morning but will now be added to your database.

Next, **follow up** by texting or calling the people whose business card you collected. Remind them where and how you met, invite them to opt-into your neighbourhood nurturer. That will keep them up to date with how the real estate market is behaving in their area—everyone loves this. Don't forget, ask them for a referral and remind them that you'll be following up quarterly and checking in. Set aside a block of time in your daily calendar to follow up with all the people whose cards you collected. It doesn't matter when—just make sure it's a non-negotiable blocked into your schedule.

The goal of this process is to **set an appointment** to go see your new contacts. Perhaps give them a home evaluation or take them out for a coffee and turn them into raving fans of YOU as an individual. You don't need to do a transaction with someone to have them be a lead magnet for your business. Get them to appreciate you for how you show up, your character, your honesty and your integrity. Once that appointment is locked into your schedule, it's another non-negotiable.

And now we come to **scripting and role-playing**. You should be joining a scripting group every day—any time from 7:00 am to 9:00 am, for fifteen to thirty minutes. Here's where you get to practice what you expect to hear when you're out, how you will respond and build the confidence you need to handle objections.

And not having a group is not an excuse; Top Producers call agents from different cities, from different non-competing states and provinces and they build their own high-level, high-achieving, scripting and masterminding group. This is where they get to practice and build up the skills they need to have great conversations, drive more leads to their database, and have more follow-ups so they can book more appointments and negotiate contracts that build the business and thus the life they know they can have!

Document your processes

An indispensable task for Top Producers is the meticulous documentation of their processes. Leveraging applications like Notion, Monday.com, or the reliable Google Docs is highly effective. In concise point form and using brief descriptions, this documentation becomes the blueprint for operational excellence.

And what should you document? I'm glad you asked. At Vaughan Real Estate Advisers, we have developed playbooks and operational manuals covering various aspects of our business, including:

- The VREA Showing Process
- The VREA Listing Presentation Process
- The VREA Leasing Process
- Daily Activities of a VREA Listing Agent
- Daily Activities of a VREA Marketing Coordinator

These manuals and playbooks are important investments. They serve as invaluable tools for presenting to your team, and as foundational resources for onboarding new members. Moreover, they play a key role in maintaining accountability within the team, ensuring that everyone aligns with the established processes and practices.

Now, try not to be overwhelmed by the idea of creating these documents. You don't have to create dozens of volumes of detailed procedures right off the bat. After all, you're not running a multi-billion-dollar empire with legal departments and 500 employees—yet! So, take a breath and listen to my advice. Here's the great thing about this—all these manuals and playbooks can be done in point form on a simple Word document. And remember—it's a LIVING document. As you grow, as your business grows, as new procedures come into play, as your governing bodies change rules and regulations, your playbooks and operations manuals will change—and this is OKAY! You can easily adapt and add to your documents as you go. Start small and simple, and as your business grows, so will your standard process documents.

Don't make it difficult—make the review process fun. Once a month, think about how you do things and how you can improve your procedures and update your documents. You can simply take screen shots and then describe what it is that you see so others can easily understand.

Get on top of accounting and taxes

I may not be an accountant, but I know that the significance of understanding numbers, taxes, fund allocation, and meticulous financial management in sales cannot be overstated.

For a top-producing agent, staying abreast of all financial aspects of their business dealings is critical to maintaining a high level of client service. Hiring the necessary expertise to keep your books clean and organized is paramount. Allocate thirty minutes every week to organize receipts, check finances for profitability, and ensure everything is prepared for income tax purposes and sales tax filings.

Top Producers run a profitable business, they're in control of their expenses. A profitable business is one where the revenue is greater than the expenses. A REAL Top Producer is meticulous with their finances and, most importantly, they understand that without controlling their finances there is NO business. They are merely doing a JOB that will eventually not be able to support their lack of good financial judgements and habits.

There are a few places you should be looking to keep organized:

- Physical Receipts—*In the shoe box*
- Credit Card Statements—*Print them & audit them*
- E-receipts—*Print them and keep them*

Let me tell you a little about how I learned to stay on top of my paperwork when I was starting out...

Every day, I would put all the physical receipts I had in a shoe box—yes, a shoe box. At the end of the month, I would pull the receipts out, and staple and separate them as my accountant recommended: business meetings, gas, car expenses, educational, stationery, client gifts, and so on. Speak to your accountant about how they would like you to do this. Then I would put the organized receipts aside along with the credit card statement for that month.

Next, I would pull together all my transaction records sheets and put them in that month's folder. This was sufficient for my accountant to tell me how much sales tax I owed, how much income tax I would need to be putting aside in a savings account, and what my profit and loss statement would look like each month so that I could see if my business was operating at a profit. If not, I had some work to do—tweaking expenses and activities.

Now, I am certain there are apps that work better nowadays, but these methods were simple and effective. Everything was super tidy and organized, making it easy to submit everything to my accountant twelve times a year.

The key takeaway here is not the details involved in accomplishing these tasks, but the imperative to schedule a meeting with an accountant. A professional accountant can assist in setting up your finances and clarifying where every dollar is allocated. You need an accountant who can advise you. A REAL Top Producer is always well-supported by great legal advisors who help to keep the business running smoothly and out of the weeds.

It's also crucial to recognize that not all income is personal profit. The commission earned is your company's revenue. Out of this revenue, a predetermined amount is designated for your compensation—a figure best determined in consultation with your accountant.

Establishing a systematic approach, designed to run seamlessly and automatically, saves valuable thinking time and minimizes the worry and stress that can be associated with finances. This approach lets you focus more on delivering exceptional service to your clients and rewarding yourself and your family with stress-free, quality time.

CHAPTER SUMMARY

At its core, sales is the essence of our profession—after all, we are salespeople. However, it is essential to view each "sale" not just as the conclusion, but as the commencement of a transformative journey for you and your business.

The impact of one sale extends far beyond immediate financial gains. It's the moment to begin cultivating good habits, and should prompt you to document essential processes and lay the foundation for a systematic approach to running your business. Systems and processes are not just for agents achieving lofty transaction numbers. Start thinking like a REAL Top Producer from the first sale.

While sales are undeniably the lifeblood of financial stability, they are also the base upon which your systems and processes are built. Do not underestimate the importance of systemizing your business. Strong systems and processes free your mind to focus on more important activities. Whether you're just starting out or well into dozens of sales per month, the imperative is clear—initiate the integration of systems and processes now. The future prosperity of your business hinges on this.

6 🔑 TAKEAWAYS

- It's important to make the shift from sales to systematic documentation by creating an Operations Manual with SOPs and processes.

- Integrating systems that align with defined processes will enhance operational efficiency and ensure that you are running a PROFITABLE business.

- Initiating the development of processes and systems early in the life of your business will save time and prevent rework when you have an even bigger business.

- Focusing on fundamental tasks such as lead generation, follow-up, negotiation, scripted role-playing, and consistent scheduling will lead to sustained success.

- Accounting and taxes are important areas of the business and you should dedicate a block of time to filing receipts each week.

- A professional accountant can provide clarity on your business finances, and also give you peace of mind.

ARE YOU A **REAL** TOP PRODUCER?

Find out:

Get your RTP Rating now! Take the assessment to find out
if you are currently a REAL Top Producer, and if not, what
you're missing to get there:

chrischopite.com/REALTopProducer/Assessment

CHAPTER 8

TRACKING ACTIVITIES & NUMBERS

*"Motivation is like bathing; you have
to do it every day, or else you stink."*

ZIG ZIGLAR
Influential American author, salesman
and motivational speaker

ONE OF the most challenging tasks on the road to becoming a REAL Top Producer is consistently tracking your activities and business numbers. As someone who has coached hundreds of agents, I've observed that there's a lot of reluctance to do these activities. Still, their impact on gauging the trajectory of your business and the likelihood of achieving your goals is immense. According to Jake Dixon, the founder of Locker Room Coaching, which serves over 3,000 real estate professionals, "You can't improve what you can't measure." Committing to daily activity tracking sends a powerful message about your responsibility and dedication to doing what's necessary for success. It signifies a refusal to hide from shortcomings, demonstrating that you are in control of your actions and accountable for your results. And neglecting to track numbers has the opposite effect.

I get that you probably don't want to talk about this subject, let alone commit to doing it, but a REAL Top Producer doesn't make excuses. A REAL Top Producer draws inspiration from acting with integrity every day. They engage in the right activities, diligently track results, and conduct weekly analyses to identify areas for improvement.

Tracking and transparency— your secret weapon

Let me share a funny observation about tracking numbers and activity...

Through my coaching experiences and interactions with numerous agents, I've noticed that those who neglect to input their numbers are often concealing shortcomings. It's a sign of their consistent lack of effort, highlighting an inability to focus on crucial tasks, a lack of self-discipline, and a failure to execute the activities necessary to reach their goals.

These agents frequently lack essential components in their business plan. Their goals lack ambition, they lack a compelling WHY and, most significantly, they succumb to the distraction of the mundane issues of everyday life—whether it's a call from the phone company about late payments or assisting a friend with a bathroom project. These distractions keep them tethered to an average producer role, preventing them from becoming a REAL Top Producer in their own right.

Statistics reveal a clear correlation: those who don't track their work often aren't doing it. Furthermore, if the work isn't done, their financial responsibilities—monthly fees, licensing costs and general life expenses—become burdensome. As a result, agents may settle for regular jobs, adopt a dual-career model, or exit the industry altogether.

Commitment to activity tracking is a leading indicator of your future career trajectory. As a coach, I closely monitor this, along with attendance to coaching calls, and this monitoring allows me to predict, with remarkable accuracy, who possesses the mindset, commitment and determination to evolve into a REAL Top Producer.

By now, you're probably wondering, "But Chris, which activities do I track?" I'm glad you asked. You want data you can use for projections, improvement and checking your progress.

Let's dive into it!

Activities to track for success

As a real estate professional, constructing and maintaining your database, often called your "databank," is paramount. It serves as the bedrock from which all your finances, business and opportunities come. To ensure the vitality of this crucial asset, Top Producers meticulously track the following fundamental elements daily:

Key trackable business activities

Conversations	Two-way communication, where at some point real estate was discussed, at the very least ending with a request for a referral.
Database ads	How many leads have you added to your database today—you must have a name, number and email. The address is preferred, but optional.
Calls made	The number of dials you made today.
Doors knocked	The number of doors you knocked on today.
Appointments booked	The number of appointments you booked today.
Appointments completed	The number of appointments that you WENT ON, not the appointments booked.
Roleplay or scripting sessions	This is the practice session that prepares you for a successful day. It's an activity that is sometimes taken very lightly, but has one of the biggest upsides—it's the way you start your engines. Do you want them warm? Or do you want a cold start?

Certainly, there are additional components you can incorporate into your tracker to enhance your business. REAL Top Producers go beyond the fundamental activities listed above; they dedicate time to bolstering their branding, ensuring they remain front-of-mind for everyone in their database. Leveraging technology and social media, they strategically remind people of their presence. Here are other elements you should consider tracking on a daily or weekly basis:

Optional metrics for your business

Social media lives or videos posted	You should be engaging your audience at least once per week—reminding them you're in the business and ready to help them when they're ready.
Handwritten notes	This represents a significant untapped potential in today's real estate landscape. While many prefer the convenience of texting and emailing, solely relying on technology aligns you with the masses. Top Producers recognize the importance of standing out, and leverage simple yet impactful gestures like handwritten notes to capture more of their clients' mindshare.
Coffee dates and lunches	Friends, BE HUMAN—grab a coffee and meet up with your core advocates and vendor partners—here's a chance for you to be "normal." Invite them out and talk about their life; be confident and lend an ear. One of my mentors told me, "Everyone has a story to tell, and no one to tell it to—be that person who is interested in people and, in return, they will be devoted to you and your mission."

Numbers and the business side

Buyer appointments completed	Simple: how many and when do you go on a buyer appointment? Track it and log it.
Buyer contracts signed	When you sign the Buyer Agreement—track it and log it.
Buyer closing	When you have a closing from a buyer—a.k.a. a "Purchase"—track it and log it.
Seller appointments completed	How many seller appointments have you gone to?
Seller contracts signed	How many seller contracts (listing agreements) have you signed?
Seller closing	Track when the property is closed for your seller client.
Volume closed	The dollar amount of the sale or purchase closed on that day.

The items listed above are important to track. While there's more you can include in your tracker, the key is that Top Producers consistently monitor their own or their team's activities and business metrics. They understand their numbers and study them for improvements, providing a clear reference point for business direction. To assist, we've developed a comprehensive activity and business tracker, available for download at chrischopite.com/RTP, complete with instructions on set-up and usage.

How to track your activities and numbers

So, let's talk about the tracker. Your tracker doesn't have to be COMPLEX and hard to use. In fact, it NEEDS to be easy to access, user friendly and accurate. The tracker we use is called the RealStat Tracker and we use it for all our coaching clients. It's a custom spreadsheet used to track our activities that we have developed over time based on the output we need to see daily, weekly, monthly, quarterly and yearly.

For my coaching clients, the routine involves logging into their trackers after the workday, typically at 9:00 pm when lead-generating activities are no longer feasible. They systematically log in and upload their daily numbers at this designated time, ensuring a consistent and structured approach to tracking their activities.

Below is an image of the tracker we use to keep track of our activities daily.

DAILY							
ACTIVITIES							
Day # (Weekly Target)	5 Conversations / Day (25)	Doors Knocked (125)	Coffee or Lunch (2)	FB Live or IG Story (1)	Handwritten Notes (10)	Script Practice (5)	Database Ads (5)
1	5	0	1	2	2	1	5
2	2	0	0	1	2	1	5
3	15	27	1	0	2	1	7
4	8	50	2	0	2	1	8
5	5	25	1	1	5	1	3
6	20	80	1	0	10	1	9
7	3	0	0	2	1	1	1

FIGURE 8.1 The daily tracker

We also have tabs that show the total numbers so we can review them and see what the month looks like, and also what each quarter looks like.

MONTHLY	5 Conversations / Day (25)	Doors Knocked (125)	Coffee or Lunch (2)	FB Live or IG Story (1)	Handwritten Notes (10)	Script Practice (5)	Database Ads (5)
January	183	420	10	6	42	20	31
February	213	383	8	8	30	20	23
March	201	390	7	6	38	20	33

FIGURE 8.2 The monthly to quarterly tracker

If you want to explore all the features of our tried-and-true activity tracker, or better yet, start using it, head to chrischopite.com/RTP and download it for free and edit it as you see fit. You'll also find a video explanation that will go along with the tracker so you know exactly how to use it for your real estate business. Every business will track slightly different things, but the important thing is to get started.

Turbocharge your tracking with a HOT List

Okay, that's the basics of tracking covered. Now let's take it a step further. A super important daily activity is to check your "HOT LIST." If you close a sale with the people on this list, you would accomplish your Gross Commission Income (GCI) or financial goals. It's important to keep a hot list and be aware of the potential revenue that the clients on that list can bring in—this is a great motivational tool. Although revenue should NOT be the primary reason for providing your service, it would be absurd to not recognize that there is a financial reward on the other side of your efforts.

The hot list can be a tab on your activity tracker that shows the name, approximate purchase price or sale price, and the approximate GCI that that transaction would yield. At the end you can add all this all together to show the GCI potential for the current hot list. Keep this list moving, add people to it, and do your job by finding a home for these people or selling their home and moving them off this list ASAP so you can stay on track with your financial objectives.

Here's an example of a typical "HOT LIST":

2024 Hot List

Client Name	Transaction Type	Approximate Volume	Pre-Approved	Appointment Attended	Contract Signed	Potential GCI
Mary J.	Seller	$825,000	Seller	Yes	Yes	$16,500
Fatima J. Anwar A.	Seller	$615,000	Seller	Yes	No	$12,300
Eva G.	Seller	$780,000	Seller	Yes	No	$15,600
	Buyer	$800,000	Yes	Yes	No	$20,000
Carlos V.	Seller	$1,260,000	Seller	Yes	No	$25,200
Lorena G.	Seller	$2,000,000	Seller	No	No	$40,000

FIGURE 8.3 The HOT list

In our coaching program, both in our group coaching and in my one-on-one program, we use a spreadsheet that tracks all activities, from conversations to scripting calls, and all the way to a GCI. We also include which properties are closing, the addresses and closing dates.

Within our group coaching program, we strive to make the tracker simple to use but super-efficient. During the day, all members of my coaching program are encouraged to keep track of conversations and anything they do in whatever way works for them. For example, I have a few clients that walk around with a piece of paper and just do ticks, then at the end of the day they input the final numbers.

The goal is to have all your activities and numbers ready to plug into the tracker at 9:00 pm. And there's a reason for this. At 9:00 pm, in most cases, the house is wound down, the kids are in bed (maybe not sleeping) but in bed, you've eaten dinner, and very likely all your work is completed for the day. Even if you're in the middle of an offer, there is some down time between negotiations and you can find five to ten minutes to input your numbers so you don't lose momentum in your business.

Go to www.chrischopite.com/RTP/Tools to get an example of what an activity and business tracker should look like. We also have one you can use yourself to track your numbers and daily metrics

CHAPTER SUMMARY

Top Producers understand that tracking their activities and business essentials is non-negotiable. It's the "air" their business breathes. While business planning is inspiring, this activity tracking is, for most people, well . . . just boring and tedious. But this is where the magic unfolds; without it, the business halts. Overcoming activity challenges requires personal motivation. While processes and systems can be taught, the hunger to succeed must come from within. As Les Brown emphasizes, "You gotta be HUNGRY!" Being hungry means relentless pursuit, a trait REAL Top Producers embody. The formula is simple: do your work, track it, and be a Top Producer.

6 🔑 TAKEAWAYS

- Inspect what you expect—you MUST track your activities so you can ensure you're on pace to reach your yearly, monthly and daily goals.

- Track your business—this will allow you to see what you've done during the year and analyze where your gaps are.

- It's important to review your goals in the morning and at night. Start the day by reviewing the metrics you must hit, and finish the day by inputting your numbers and ending the day on a small "win."

- There are many ways to track your activities and your business—you can use different software, spreadsheets, or even a white board to start. But I highly recommended you track your activities using software once you're up and running. REAL Top Producers leverage technology into their business!

- Create a HOT list—look at it daily, let it motivate you, and make sure to turn it into a revolving door. In and out you go! On the list and SOLD or BOUGHT!

- REAL Top Producers keep track of their business. They know their numbers and they enjoy looking at their daily wins, because they know that daily wins will stack up to massive victories.

ARE YOU A **REAL** TOP PRODUCER?

Find out:

Get your RTP Rating now! Take the assessment
to find out if you are currently a REAL Top Producer,
and if not, what you're missing to get there:

chrischopite.com/REALTopProducer/Assessment

CHAPTER 9

PRODUCTIVITY & GROWTH

"Success is the peace of mind which is a direct result of self-satisfaction in knowing you did your best to become the best that you are capable of becoming."

JOHN WOODEN
American ten-time NCAA championship
basketball coach (UCLA) and creator
of The Pyramid of Success

THE TIME has come to turbocharge your business. You've laid a solid foundation, created a business based on that foundation, and begun the process of elevating your business by establishing systems and processes and learning to track your activities and numbers. This final chapter is where the rubber hits the road—where you will learn how to boost your productivity and grow your business beyond the basics and into the realm of a REAL Top Producer.

In this chapter we're going to dive into some tips and tricks to help you maximize productivity, then we'll get into accountability partnerships before deep-diving into how a winning team is built.

Productivity—the Holy Grail

Here's the thing about productivity; there's no *one* thing you can do to be more productive. Productivity is a build-up of many things you do that, collectively, make you more productive.

I'd say productivity starts with the mindset that you should never be satisfied with everything your business does at any given moment. In business, what you did to get HERE will not get you THERE (wherever there is). You must constantly improve, and part of this improvement is looking for strategies to become more productive.

Productivity is a constant pursuit—you will never arrive at a destination where you are the most productive you can possibly be. There will always be ways to improve your productivity because new platforms, apps and tools are launched in the world of technology all the time. As your business faces fresh challenges in an ever-evolving industry, you will find that you simply don't have the know-how to overcome them. The only way to stay efficient and become more productive is to hire someone who knows all about whatever hurdle your business is facing.

Time or money?

Improving productivity means doing more in less time. It also means doing the same thing better so that you attract more business instead of having to hunt for it. But another way to think of productivity is to do what you're doing, but gradually do less and less of it so that your business can support the life you want to live.

| CURRENT OUTPUT | $100k IN 60 HRS/WEEK |

OPTIONS FOR PRODUCTIVITY	$100k IN 40 HRS/WEEK
	$140k IN 60 HRS/WEEK
	$80k IN 0 HRS/WEEK

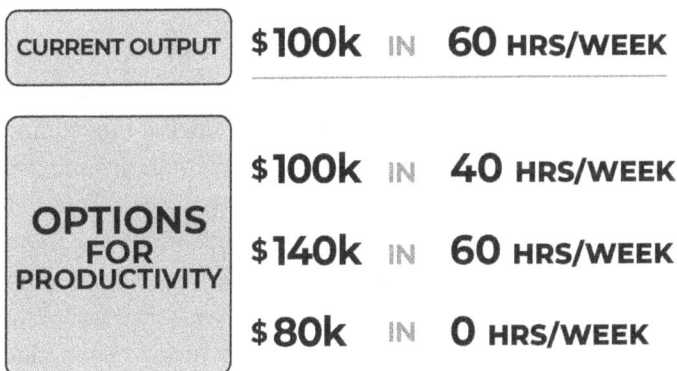

FIGURE 9.1 Example of productivity in numbers

For example, let's say you made $100,000 in a year, but you worked sixty hours a week to accomplish that. Well, in order to be more productive, you would need to employ people or methods that will make $100,000 for you in forty hours (twenty fewer than before) or make $140,000 in sixty hours. Or you could aim for your business to make a little less for you—say $80,000—but with zero hours put in by you. This would allow you to do whatever you want in life; spend more time with your kids, spend more time playing sports and working out, and so on.

Of course, this requires you to know what you want. If you haven't put some effort into following the advice in Parts 1 and 2 of this book and try to jump right into this section, you will face some frustrating challenges. Not to say that it can't be done, but skipping steps along the way could cause you some great setbacks and discomfort. The best way to be productive is to start with a strong foundation, great habits and the right mindset. Then, and ONLY THEN, can you improve and add measures to increase your production or productivity.

Beware of hyper productivity

Okay, now I'm going to contradict myself—kinda. There is such a thing as TOO MUCH productivity. People who are hyper-productive are in danger of spending all their time developing systems, but failing to use them to accomplish their goals because they're obsessed with making them better and better. Systems are useless if you don't use them. You improve systems as you deploy them into the market. If you fall in the hyper-productive pocket, you may fail to take action and therefore won't get any results. Then, due to the lack of results (which you should not be focused on in the first place), you'll struggle to keep your mental state positive (you're human, after all) and this will lead you into a massive unproductive slide and then you'll get depressed.

So how do you avoid falling into hyper-productivity and becoming this person who is constantly seeking ways to do things easier, faster and better?

First, remember that it's not always going to look like it's working. Just because you're not getting results right off the bat, doesn't mean that your marketing, your efforts, your door knocking, your cold calling and your impact are not being felt. Every marketing campaign needs time to develop, and small adjustments will always be necessary. But jumping from one bait to the next isn't always ideal as you will be spending more time changing directions than marketing to your audience. A REAL Top Producer knows this. They understand that when results don't come immediately, you shouldn't abandon your plan and go back to the drawing board to create another one. Stick with it and give it time to work. And be careful about the social media you consume; beware of alleged time-management gurus trying to sell you a productivity hack that will make all your challenges go away in a click of the mouse. You have to be mentally ready to have the self-discipline to stick to the plan without being sidetracked.

Of course, it's possible that there IS a better way, and you just don't know about it. As tools develop there will always be a better way. As agents and Top Producers, our job is to sell and research. But we can't always focus on just researching the latest trends and tools. Stay attentive to the shifts in the industry, but always remain focused on completing your tasks. Any changes you make should be small tweaks and made quarterly.

Something else you can do to fight through the feeling of not getting results fast enough is to revisit your goals. If you're WAY off track, then you need to review your strategies. In most cases your goal and your priorities are okay, and it's the strategies that need to be looked at in depth. But you should only be retooling them quarterly—if you're constantly adjusting, then you're doing it wrong. If you need to make changes, apply the tweaks, then revisit your numbers after ninety days and check how things are going compared to the last ninety days.

And if you haven't set your goals and built your plan, go back and read Part 1: Sacrifice and Courage. Build your plan and learn how to master your time. Why? Because at some point you need to realize that ALL that you can do is lead with sacrifice and courage, build a plan of action and then execute it.

Partner up to power up

All the most accomplished individuals in the world emphasize the importance of having not just one, but multiple coaches. My good friend and business partner Sandy MacKay aptly refers to us as corporate athletes. Aiming to be a REAL Top Producer requires adopting the mindset of hall-of-famers in the corporate athletic world. Accountability, support, shortcuts, training and consultants are crucial to achieving and sustaining performance. I engage with both a business coach and a real estate coaching coach, and each serves a distinct purpose. One coaches me on overall business practice and mastering the art of being a founder and Key Person of Influence, and the other guides me on how to coach real estate professionals to their highest and best self. Additionally, I maintain mentors from diverse backgrounds to provide different perspectives and opinions, ensuring my decisions consider multiple approaches and potential outcomes.

As a coach, trainer, consultant, and public speaker, there are many areas of my career where I always need to be improving. Next up for me will be improving my presentation skills and finding a coach or consultant who can guide me to better practices. These coaches and mentors not only help me to improve my skills, they also hold me accountable to the activities that I must do in order to achieve the objectives I've set out for myself!

Accountability partners—Who are they, and what do they do for you?

Accountability partners, such as coaches, consultants, advisers and mentors, provide insights, advice, and accountability. Understanding who they are, what they do for you, and when to seek their assistance can supercharge your journey toward success. Let's look at the diverse roles of these accountability partners, and explore their unique contributions and the scenarios where their expertise can be invaluable.

Coaches

You can be coached in many areas of your life: personal, business and fitness. Coaches will ask questions, actively listen and give advice. They suggest strategies that best suit you based on the goals you're trying to achieve. Coaches are more of a long-term relationship—they help you create a schedule, stay on top of your game, attack the strategy, and hold you accountable.

Consultants

Consultants solve problems; they advise on particular details. You can have marketing consultants, branding consultants or even database management consultants. The big one is business consultants, who can help you build a business, direct the executive team to best practices, and ensure high level advice for the core team. Consultants are usually hired for a term. They're there to consult on a particular challenge, help to solve it, and put a solution and a system in place; the support usually stops there.

Advisers

Advisers can share insight based on experience. They give suggestions but are involved at a distance, on an as-needed basis.

Mentors

Mentors are active listeners, and mentors must choose you; you don't choose your mentor. The nature of the mentor is to give; you must listen and accept the information they're giving. Usually, a mentor has been or is where you want to be. Mentors will hold you accountable—they want their advice taken seriously and applied conscientiously.

Build your WINNING Team

Tracking your numbers and sticking to a great marketing plan are key for productivity. The other secret weapon is having the right people in your business. Your winning team is made up of the people in your world who will allow you to grow into something unique. As you build your team and create winning systems and models, your team will adapt to your current strategies. And, here's the big one—adopt new strategies to improve on what you originally thought were the best processes.

Hiring for your business is akin to building your all-star team. Unlike your accountability network, you have more control over who is on your court when hiring. The decision to hire support is pivotal, but it's crucial to dispel the notion that it grants you a year-long vacation or exempts you from work. Contrary to this misconception, hiring is not a ticket to idleness but signifies a shift in your responsibilities. This transition doesn't grant you the luxury of complete detachment from your professional life. Instead, it demands a change in your role. It's not about ceasing all activity; it's about altering your focus and responsibilities. It all comes down to productivity gain.

Hiring is a critical decision that warrants careful consideration, whether bringing on staff members and new agents or engaging in partnerships with marketing companies and collaborators. The adage "hire slow and fire fast" is wise. When I reflect on my own experiences, I can see when I've mistakenly hired individuals, without a clear purpose or structured process. There was an absence of checklists, accountability measures, and a 30–60–90 day game plan. This led to keeping unsuitable team members on board for extended periods, because I couldn't face the stress of finding replacements, and it cost me tens of thousands of dollars. However, the hard-learned lesson led me to develop a comprehensive hiring process and a swift termination formula, safeguarding both the company's time and the individuals involved.

If someone doesn't align with your organization, it's in everyone's best interests to part ways and allow them to find a more suitable fit elsewhere. Collaborating with individuals within your organization should not be burdensome; instead, they should actively contribute to lightening your workload and consistently seek ways to alleviate work pressures.

When assembling your team, choose individuals whose values align with your own. The Leverage Series offered by Keller Williams University is an excellent resource for gaining a deeper understanding of hiring, firing, and fostering growth within your team. This course is accessible to any agent and provides valuable insights into effective team management.

When and who to hire

The hires that I believe are super important are: an administrative assistant, a marketing manager, and, finally, a salesperson. And you should hire them in this order. No other order works—change it and you will fail. I've seen this happen over and over again.

In the book *The Millionaire Real Estate Agent*, Gary Keller talks about how important it is to hire administrative help first. This strategic move is your gateway to liberating yourself from daily tasks, allowing a qualified professional to handle operational details. It allows you to redirect your focus toward the vital twenty percent of activities that drive the core of your business. Think about it. At first you're a solo agent, working hard, doing everything; then, as you grow your business, you hire someone who can help you with the paperwork, your calendar, receipts, organizing your files and emails. With all this paperwork taken off your hands, you now have the time to get more business.

You should consider making this crucial hire during the BPM stage, and you should also be clear about just what your EA should be doing. They SHOULD be managing your calls, scheduling your appointments and sending emails.

They should NOT be creating social media posts, doing cold calls or any other tasks that require real estate knowledge and training.

My executive assistant is an extension of everything in my life. She overlooks all my emails, ensures I stay on top of all my tasks, ensures my calendar is properly synched with all my family responsibilities, and pulls me out of trouble when I need to find documents and present to business partners or teach at a different brokerage. But her most important role is planning and organizing our weeks and months to stay ahead and on track with our annual goals.

For a comprehensive understanding of the transformative impact an executive assistant can have, check out the insights offered by *The Founder and the Force Multiplier*. This enlightening read provides invaluable lessons on the business of hiring, guiding you in selecting and leveraging talent to fortify your business foundation.

The next hire on your list, I believe, should be a marketing manager. This can be done at different stages, but the short answer on when to do it is when you've grown the business to the point that you have the revenue to do it.

In today's industry, where content creation and the way you market yourself to the public is so important, this makes sense. When you hire a marketing manager you can reallocate the time saved to building a leads funnel that brings in more business than you can handle... THEN, and only then, you hire a salesperson to help you work the business that you don't have the time to do anyway. See how this works? The admin and marketing help frees up your time to bring in more leads, and once you have leads coming out of your ears, you need someone to help sell the listings that are piling up.

This is the most organic, smart and logical way to grow into a small and powerful real estate company.

Let's finish up by looking at another of my cute diagrams, which gives you a visual representation of an ideal growth path where you're growing through/with people.

EARN $180,000+

3RD HIRE
SALESPERSON OR SHOWING ASSISTANT

1ST HIRE
ADMINISTRATIVE ASSISTANT

2ND HIRE
MARKETING MANAGER

BRING ON A COACH
BUILD YOUR ADVISORY TEAM

THIS WILL HELP NAVIGATE CHALLENGES

EARN $80,000 - $120,000
LEAN INTO YOUR BROKERAGE AND GROUP COACHING

TOP PRODUCER **TEAM BUILDING PROGRESS CHART**

FIGURE 9.2 How to grow a winning team

CHAPTER SUMMARY

The key to recapturing your time lies in increasing productivity and building your winning team. When it comes to productivity, know that you're playing the long game. You must be patient. Partnering with the right people will enhance your growth. As the business grows, you no longer have to go at it alone. When the time is right, start building your team. With the right personnel, you can redirect your focus to other important things: family vacations, inspiring others, or community involvement. Building a team of highly efficient, motivated individuals aligned with your team or organization's big goals ensures lasting success in your real estate business.

6 🔑 TAKEAWAYS

🔓 Increased productivity is the Holy Grail that will free up your time for meaningful activities—time with family, vacations, self-care, to name a few.

🔓 Beware the hyper-productivity trap. Don't get so caught up in refining your systems and processes that they don't have time to work.

🔓 Coaches, consultants, advisers and mentors can guide your personal and professional development journey and ensure you remain accountable.

🔓 Hiring is not a ticket to idleness. Instead, it signifies a shift in responsibilities, emphasizing ongoing commitment and involvement.

🔓 Hiring must be done in the right order. Strategically replace roles, starting with administrative positions, followed by a marketing manager, followed by a new salesperson, using a dynamic "wheel of replacement."

🔓 Recapturing time is achieved through strategic hiring and leadership, redirecting focus toward impactful activities, and seeking expert advice for efficient team building.

ARE YOU A **REAL** TOP PRODUCER?

Find out:

Get your RTP Rating now! Take the assessment
to find out if you are currently a REAL Top Producer,
and if not, what you're missing to get there:

chrischopite.com/REALTopProducer/Assessment

CONCLUSION
INSPIRE OTHERS

"Strive not to be successful,
but to be of value."

ALBERT EINSTEIN
Renowned theoretical physicist,
creator of the theory of relativity and
author of the equation E=mc²

FRIEND, IT has been an incredible journey together, and I feel truly privileged to have shared this space with you. By now, you possess the invaluable secrets and knowledge required to become a REAL Top Producer and continue excelling in that role.

I hold dear our connection throughout this book, and I sincerely wish to serve as an ongoing source of inspiration for you.

Together we have explored the foundations necessary to uphold your expansive life, gaining a profound understanding of commitment and sacrifice. You've learned the art of creating a precise plan, ensuring a clear, manageable and executable roadmap. You know how to optimize your twenty-four hours and turn the tables so that life works for you, not against you.

Once the foundational groundwork was laid, you discovered how to elevate your BPM and infuse vibrancy into your business soundtrack. The journey involved perfecting your branding, enhancing your presence, and consistently being a force whenever you step into a room. Collaborating with professionals and experts allows you to master marketing, attract your ideal clientele, and establish a business that aligns with your significant WHY.

The significance of tracking your numbers and activities became evident and you learned that what isn't measured cannot be analyzed and improved. Next the game-changer was revealed—that hiring coaches, consultants and educators is the biggest cheat code in human history. Introducing accountability through these guiding figures emerged as a surefire way to secure shortcuts to success.

Documenting and organizing your models, systems, processes, sales strategies, lead-generation methods, marketing approaches, training manuals, and all the fine details for your working life became crucial. You acknowledged that these documents are living, breathing entities that should evolve with market changes. As a leader and Top Producer, you know that these activities should be second nature to you and this will set the tone for the entire team.

Transitioning from operational systems to hiring marks a pivotal moment when you reclaim your time. Human resources become more manageable with everything meticulously documented and structured. The beauty lies in having already envisioned your path and battle-tested your models. Now, you're ready to bring on the team that will elevate your business to unparalleled heights.

As you welcome the right people on board, your role transforms into that of "Lead Inspirationalist" within your team and organization. Now is your time to illuminate others, share more of yourself, and give, inspire and motivate everyone to new heights.

This is your last step to becoming a REAL Top Producer. Now is your time to inspire others through everything you do and everything you've learned in this book. I encourage you to leave the world in a better state than you found it. Be a good person, do good, and be aware that others and the creator within us observe our actions. The ultimate sign of respect is striving to create a positive impact in the world.

Here is my last piece of advice to you as a Top Producer, but more importantly as a leader: go forth confidently and purposefully. These are the values that should guide every decision as you jump into your journey to level up your business:

- **Your body is a temple**: Treat your body respectfully, acknowledging its power in inspiring others. Regular exercise is a duty.

- **Breathe air into the room**: Add positivity wherever you go, contributing to joy.

- **Protect the weak**: Stand up for the less fortunate and fight for those who need it most.

- **Be openly grateful**: Express gratitude consistently, letting others know you appreciate, love and admire them.

- **Learn to teach**: Master the information you learn well enough to teach and inspire others to seek knowledge.

- **Use money as a tool**: Employ money as a tool to reach more people, try new things, bring people together, and create a quality life.

- **Build better people**: Start with your children, teaching them valuable life lessons early, and lead with honesty, trust and strength.

Armed with the knowledge of inspiring others and living an inspirational life, embrace the role of REAL Top Producer—what you were born to be. Utilize the principles above to cultivate better individuals within your organization, community and family. This journey of giving, driven by shared principles, is the essence of being a REAL Top Producer—living a life of inspiration for others, not just oneself.

Before we part ways, there is one more concept I want you to embrace—to believe in yourself, believe in others, and allow others to believe in you. When you believe in you, others believe in you, and you believe in others, magic happens. Imagine it like a Venn diagram—a BELIEVENN diagram—where the intersection of these three passionate beliefs creates a sweet spot at the centre where the highest forms of energy is produced, leading to a euphoric feeling of excitement and contentment...

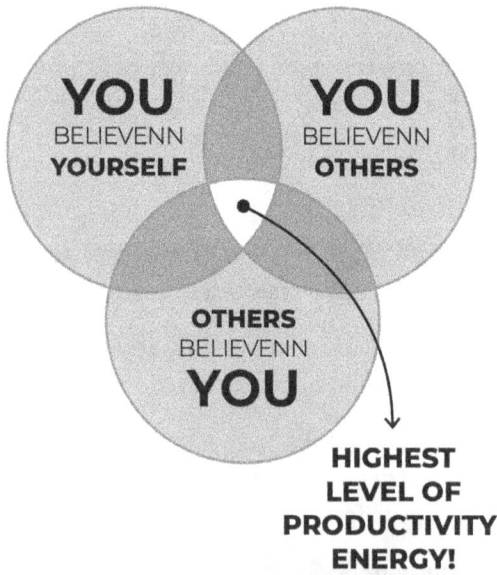

FIGURE 10.1 The BelieVENN diagram

A REAL Top Producer is: an inspirational force. Here's to your continued success and the extraordinary journey ahead.

Be Courageous.
Create Quality.
Live Inspired.

BONUS
VISUALIZATION
EXERCISE

ONE OF the most powerful forces in your journey to success is the practice of visualization. In Chapter 2 we talked about how to create a vision and mission board. Another way to harness the power of visualization is through the formal practice of visualizing your future. Below is a transcript you can use to practice visualization regularly. You can find a recording of this at chrischopite.com/RTP, but if you prefer not to listen to me, you might like to record the words below in your own voice, or perhaps the voice of a loved one, and use that recording to guide your visualization.

When you do this exercise, make sure you can be alone and undisturbed for about twenty minutes. Lie down or sit in a comfortable chair. Take the time to do some deep breathing, light a scented candle, or do whatever you need to get into a relaxed state before you begin. Once you're ready, close your eyes, begin the recording, and give yourself over to the glorious images that form in your mind.

It's morning. You open your eyes, and lie motionless in your bed. Not because you can't get up, but because you're staring at the ceiling thinking about all the hard work you have done and how it has been worth every bead of sweat. You take a deep breath, exhale and smile. The thought, "Thank you, God," comes to mind. You sit up, you do a quarter turn, and place your feet firmly on the floor. Beneath your feet you feel the soft and cozy bristles of a beautiful area rug meticulously placed under the bed of your dreams.

You stand up and walk towards the bathroom, where you look at yourself in the mirror and smile. You're so proud of who you have become. You look into the reflection of your eyes in the mirror and you see now what a REAL Top Producer looks like. What a hard-working, brave, quality-driven and inspired business person looks like. Such a person looks like you.

As you continue with your morning routine, you go to your closet and realize that it's well organized and you have everything you need and want to make yourself look professional, comfortable, elegant and impressive. You know that if you look good you feel good, and if you feel good everything else becomes that much easier in your day-to-day life.

You dress for the day, and you're happy about your attire. It makes you feel good. It makes you feel empowered. You make your way down the stairs and you're greeted by your family—the family that you always wanted. They're happy, you're happy, and you're engulfed with joy knowing that the hard work is clearly paying off.

You make your way to the kitchen for your healthy morning routine. Now you're ready to begin your day and there is nothing that can get in the way. As you step out of your home, you look back with a smile and yell out "Have a phenomenal day!" to that family that you always wanted with that person that you've always wanted to be with.

You step into the car that you've always wanted, you put your bag down beside you on the passenger seat, you press the button to start the engine, and you're ready to embark on your journey for that day. As you drive away, you look in your rearview mirror and you see the house you always wanted. That house is now home, a home that protects your most loving experiences and highlights of your life. You turn to the road in front of you again, and you smile. You're proud of who you have become. You're a REAL Top Producer.

You turn onto the road that's going to take you to your next appointment, and you smile again because you know that the hard work that you've put in, the education that you've pursued, working to be value-centric, ethical and committed to a high standard of business, has allowed you to not think about money anymore. Money is finally the tool that helps you accomplish your dreams and impact people in the most positive way possible.

At last, you park your car and feel overjoyed yet again as you reflect that you're an example of what courage, creativity, high standards and a life of inspiration can do for a person.

You are a REAL Top Producer, and you know it, and it's time to inspire others to live their best life. Everywhere you go people look up to you. They want to know your story, they wish to be in your presence, they consider you vital to any conversation. Opportunities come to you constantly, because you improve everything you touch. Every space you walk into is filled with positive energy. You are a Top Producer and this will never change.

ACKNOWLEDGEMENTS

OUT OF the entire book, this is the toughest to write and most meaningful section for me. I'll explain shortly.

Before I say anything else... Thank you, God. Thank you for giving me the ability to fight, the wisdom to know that you are guiding me the entire way and that I have people up there with you, looking down, cheering me on and believing in me.

I'll start by thanking my family, but most importantly, my mom, for bringing me into this world. Thank you, Mom, for making the decision to come to Canada in 1992 and giving me a shot at a great life. To all my uncles, who stepped up and raised me—thank you. Thank you, Dad, Baba, for being a constant and committed figure in my life. Thank you to my Godfather, Tyrone Serrao, whose constant support, encouragement and tough love gave me perspective and built up my passion for constant improvement—thank you for all the opportunities and life experiences you have given me.

To Harold Persad, whose encouragement and mentorship propelled me to believe in myself as an entrepreneur. I doubt you fully grasp your profound impact on my journey.

Meeting you and our conversations about my future, family and business are so valuable to me, I shudder to think where I would be today without you and your support.

I extend my heartfelt appreciation to my publishing team—Scott MacMillan for believing in me more than I did. Olivia Joerges and Carolyn Jackson for diligently catching all the small errors I overlooked in my laziness, for the extra creative sessions unpacking my thoughts, and for adding a little editing brilliance to it all. This book clearly would not exist without you three, so a resounding thank you!

Now, this part is the toughest, yet the most rewarding to write. I have so many people to thank, but there are MANY that I'm sure to leave out who have impacted me in more ways than anyone could imagine. This makes this part TOUGH to write. So, I'll say: to EVERYONE who has

believed in me—all my past clients and future clients— thank you. And I cannot leave out the ones who didn't believe—know that you have impacted me in the best way possible. It was my trials and tribulations, hearing your negative thoughts, all the roadblocks you intentionally or unintentionally put in the way, and all the letdowns, that led me to where I am today. I can genuinely say, as I write this with a smile—thank you so much. You are all in my mind and in my heart, and I owe a lot of my energy and drive to you. :)

To my support team, Mike Reid and the BEQ, Jake Dixon and The Locker Room, my KW Legacies Family, especially, Sandy MacKay, Ana Marin, Martin Kuev, Zac Baker and Cynthia Gisone, you guys have believed in me, and my ability to coach, speak and impact. You have opened up the doors to a lot of my coaching opportunities and a life of impact and inspiration—thank you for giving me the opportunity to find a direction that inspires me immensely.

I want to say THANK YOU SO MUCH to everyone that took the time to read the final manuscript and drop a review. Thank you, Caffery Van Horne, not only for your review of the book but for your insight on much more. Thank you, Jay Papasan, for inspiring me with your life's work, all the books you've authored and, more importantly, for making time in your busy schedule to sit with me and instill in me some wisdom as I embarked on this exciting path of authorship and influence.

To all the agents that I've had the pleasure of coaching, thank you for allowing me to be part of your journey. A special and inspirational thanks to Sina Tahami, Eric Miraflor, Stella Ram, Oscar Romero, Mehshan Javaid, Casey Bradfield, Mohsin Lakhani, Ryan Rambocas and Vera Felice. You have all been key people and agents who have been part of great milestones in my career. Your unwavering support and alliance are priceless—as much as you think I've helped you, you'll never know the impact you had on me.

It would be impossible to close this out without huge acknowledgements to my big brother, Hossam Mostafa. You had NO IDEA that I was writing this book; I kept it from you because I wanted to surprise you, and this is how special you are to me. Thank you for EVERYTHING.

Michelle Serrao and the Intangibles team for their support throughout my business life. Josh Contreras—my guy—for your insight and creative support; I admire you and your relentless work ethic. Dustin Kuypers, from the minute we met you've been by my side, guiding my creative spirit and never letting the kid inside us die; breaking things and putting them back together; making a constant impact and not settling for normal. Thank you, my brother. Sara Munoz, for keeping me sane and on a mission—your impact in my life and that of my family is impossible to measure, and I look forward to great things together. Brian Spencer, Ivan

Birungi, Paul Attar, Jameel Rawlinson, Diogo Reis, Eric Ruiz, Hashim Arthur, David Contreras, David Peasley, Tio Orlando Diaz, Anush Pasishnik, Dean Aivaliotis, Daksh Rajwani, Alicia Erbity, Lisa Sherriff, Glenn Ting, and of course, the one and only Shanna Armogan, my sister—I love you all beyond words, and I would not even be CLOSE to where I am today without your support, encouragement and love.

Thank you to my partner in life, my rock, the woman who has seen me at my best and at my worst, the only woman brave enough to be with me. Raquel, thank you for standing steadfastly by my side throughout this journey. From the exhilarating highs of signing new clients and discovering fresh ideas to the challenging lows when faith wavered, money dwindled, and sleep eluded me. Your unwavering support has been my anchor. We have so much further to go, but I'm excited and full of joy to think of what our next chapters will look like. You're one of the most important pillars to my life and nothing would be the same without you. I love you.

You thought I'd forget? Nope. Ty, Sienna, Kiki and Z— life without you, in one word: meaningless. You have given me hope, a reason to thrive, another great reason to get up every day and push for greatness. I love watching you guys grow, learn and become the great givers that you are and will undoubtedly be when you're older. I get lost in our conversation, nothing matters, the world stops—you guys will never know how much you mean to my life. There are not enough words to describe how grateful I am for your love, your challenges and the constant pain in my a**—LOL :) Everything Daddy does is for you, to show you that anything is possible, that I will never settle and that it is important to be courageous, create quality and live inspired.

Thank you, God, for all your blessings.

ABOUT
THE AUTHOR

CHRIS CHOPITE is the founder of multiple companies, most notably Inspired Co., an organization dedicated to assisting real estate professionals in becoming Top Producers by increasing their BPM—building their brand, perfecting their presence, and mastering their market.

Chris considers his most cherished God-given gifts to be his four children. He resides in Vaughan, Ontario, with his wife Raquel and their children Ty, Sienna, Keira and Zarina.

Chris's passion for architecture began with a Certificate in Residential Design from Loyalist College and an Advanced Diploma in Architecture Technology from Humber College. He initiated his career as a Junior Architectural Designer at URS Canada Inc., an engineering and architecture firm in Markham, Ontario.

Realizing that a long corporate career was not aligned with his vision and destiny, Chris made a strategic shift. His involvement in the In-house Toastmasters at URS gave him early and mature exposure to public speaking and addressing a room.

Chris has collectively sold and bought over $100,000,000 in real estate in his career. Currently serving as a sales and marketing coach and consultant, Chris has guided hundreds of real estate professionals in understanding the essential elements of building and sustaining a robust real estate business.

Through motivational inspiration and practical models, Chris has been a driving force for many realtors, particularly during challenging market conditions. He recognizes that tough times are temporary and that calm seas don't make great sailors, so he continues to motivate and inspire.

Many of the real estate professionals coached by Chris have gone on to build successful teams, consistently close six-figure deals, or transform their careers. Chris's mission is to redefine the image of realtors, inspiring them to lead courageous lives that emit quality and inspiration. He aims to give back to an industry that has profoundly impacted his life and family.

Chris dreams of elevating the status of real estate professionals to that enjoyed by doctors, lawyers and engineers. He sees real estate as a sales job powered by education and a significant responsibility with immense emotional rewards. His goal is to reach out to realtors worldwide, guiding them to build ethical brands, exude professionalism through an elevated presence, and market themselves and their unique selling propositions to foster peace when working with clients. His vision involves empowering realtors to fight for their clients and their needs, and provide an inspiring and everlasting experience, solidifying a lasting relationship with the Top Producer.

With a foundation rooted in years of experience, Chris shows how to increase your BPM and become a REAL Top Producer, reaching undreamt of heights in the real estate industry.

From practical strategies to motivational wisdom, Chris's expertise shines through. Discover the keys to unlocking your full potential, whether you're a seasoned realtor or just starting out. Chris's mission is to redefine the realtor's image, instilling courage, quality and inspiration. Join him on this empowering journey and witness the transformation of your career and your entire real estate approach.

He is a trusted mentor with a proven track record of over $100,000,000 in real estate transactions and a top 5% ranking in Canada. As a sales and marketing coach, he has guided numerous professionals to navigate challenging market conditions, inspiring them to build robust teams and consistently earn six figures.